# PLANTING
## FOR
# GARDEN BIRDS

*1: Firecrest ♂*

# PLANTING
# FOR
# GARDEN BIRDS

## A Grower's Guide to
## Creating a Bird-Friendly Habitat

JANE MOORE

ILLUSTRATED BY JAMES WESTON LEWIS

Hardie Grant

QUADRILLE

*For* Andrew and Christina,
working in your garden
was the inspiration

# CONTENTS

*r: Robin ♂*

# INTRODUCTION

There's more to our gardens than a few pigeons. Whether they're in villages, towns or cities, all kinds of birds live in and around them, from humble House Sparrows and shy little Wrens to majestic Herons and breath-taking Peregrine Falcons. To a Peregrine, a city high-rise is ideal for nesting on, just like a cliff. The church spire close to my city home is famous for its resident Peregrines and I often hear their piercing call. There's no doubt that our homes and gardens have become increasingly important habitats for birds, even those we think of as countryside inhabitants.

Take a stroll in your local park and you'll probably see various types of Tits and Finches, perhaps a Woodpecker, or even a Kestrel or Sparrowhawk. If there's a lake or river nearby, you're likely to see Herons, Coots, Moorhens and, if you're lucky, the electric blue streak of a Kingfisher.

Some birds are residents and are around from day to day, but others are fleeting visitors, arriving purely for the summer months or passing through the garden in just a day or two. But they're all potential guests in our gardens if we make the environment suitably welcoming. That's exactly what this book is about. In these pages you'll find straightforward ideas and easy-to-achieve plans that will make your garden irresistible to birds.

The aim of this book is to broaden your knowledge and expertise, to give you ideas on planting and on how to manage your garden in a bird-friendly fashion. The planting chapters are arranged seasonally to make planning your garden easier. Your garden can be beautiful as well as bird friendly, so the plants are listed in their main season of interest for us gardeners. For instance, the Cherry is listed in spring, as that's when these beautiful trees flower, but it's mainly the late summer fruit that will attract the birds. Having said that, many plants have several seasons of interest, so I've tried to mention all of them. But it's by no means a definitive list; these are the plants that I rate as both good for birds but also as great additions to the garden.

CHAPTER ONE

# WHY GARDEN ESPECIALLY FOR BIRDS?

At first glance that's such an easy question to answer. Birds add life, colour and song to our gardens. They live their lives alongside us, eating, meeting a partner, settling down and bringing up their chicks in a parallel existence to our own. But the thing I really love about birds is the fact that many of them are with us all year round. Robins, Blackbirds, Sparrows and Dunnocks are in my garden whatever the season. Some of them, like the Robin, keep me company as I potter about the garden, especially in winter. Others, like the Sparrows, flit off chattering away as soon as I get too close. But it's the shy little Wren that really has my heart – a glimpse of this stalwart little bird hopping about busily makes me realize just how important my garden is for all the birds, including the ones I rarely see.

But, while they're beautiful to see and hear, many birds are doing quite a service for us gardeners, so it's well worth making an effort for them. Many of the most common garden birds, such as Finches and Sparrows, are seed eaters and they don't discriminate, happily eating weed seeds at a great rate and reducing the amount left to germinate. That means less weeding and no need for chemical weed killers for me. Some, such as Song Thrushes, will even tuck into slugs and snails and that's great news for every gardener.

We're so used to seeing birds all the time that we take them for granted without particularly realizing it. They're always there, all around us, flying overhead, the spring song of the Blackbird waking us up at dawn and the bold little Robin at our side looking for worms when we're gardening in the winter. I can't imagine these commonplace birds not being around – the world, let alone my garden, would be so dull and lifeless.

In recent years, we've come to realize just how important urban parks and gardens are for wildlife – they are the 'green lungs' of our towns and cities. The natural spaces our towns have to offer are increasingly becoming home to wildlife of all kinds, including birds. Many creatures are migrating into urban environments in search of food and shelter, which has become scarcer in the countryside. It doesn't matter if you make a nest on a skyscraper, office block or a cliff if you're a Peregrine Falcon, as long as it's safe, secure and close to plenty of prey. Villages, towns and cities offer an array of potential habitats, from quiet cemeteries and churchyards, with their old trees and neglected corners, to scraps of wasteland, railways lines, and even empty buildings.

There's no doubt that many common birds are threatened by various factors, among them loss of food. In 2007 the House Sparrow, Song Thrush and Starling were added as priority species to the UK Biodiversity Action Plan list. This means these once-common birds are now species to worry about. The numbers of House Sparrows, Starlings and Song Thrushes have gone down by more than half over the last 25 years. It's a similar story in the USA where breeding bird populations have dropped by 29 per cent in the past 40 years. While some of this is caused by changes in farming practices, scientists believe that the loss of insects the birds feed upon in towns and cities could also be to blame. This means we need to make sure our gardens are full of insects for birds to eat, and nothing attracts insects more than plants.

Of course, feeding birds in any way you can is paramount. Those bird feeders might feel like a miniscule effort to change things for the better, but everything has an impact. In the US,

57 million households regularly feed their local birds, while bird lovers in the UK spend more than £200 million a year on bird food, feeders and other bird paraphernalia.

While putting out food is crucial, a more holistic approach is essential to create an environment where the birds will live out their whole lives. By planting a wide range of native and bird- and insect-friendly species, you will not only attract birds to feed on the plants in your garden but insects on which many more birds will also feed. The more plants you grow, the more insects will be drawn in and so the more birds will follow. Not only that, but you won't feel the need to use insecticides as the birds will manage the insect populations for you – biological control in action.

In recent decades several big citizen science events have become annual, including the Big Garden Birdwatch, organized by the RSPB in the UK, and the Great Backyard Bird Count, headed by Audubon in the USA. Ordinary citizens have great fun recording their local birds, while providing scientists with crucial information. And initiatives like this exist all over the world. There's even a continent-wide one in the form of EuroBirdwatch, organized by BirdLife Europe and Central Asia.

Our back gardens are playing an increasingly important role. The 'green corridor' effect of hundreds of back gardens weaves its way through urban areas to open spaces such as parks, canals and rivers and then on into the wider countryside. These provide vital channels for migrating birds and insects, especially as our gardens aren't likely to be built on or suffer from the overuse of pesticides and other threats in the same way as larger open spaces. By gardening sustainably and in an environmentally conscious manner, gardeners can make a considerable difference to the wildlife populations in their immediate area, as well as the country as a whole.

It's not difficult to make your garden more bird friendly. The chances are you're already doing a lot right without realizing it: providing warmth and safety with twiggy hedges and shrubs for foliage, flowers and fruit; letting leaves that have fallen from trees and shrubs lie on the ground so that Dunnocks and Blackbirds can scratch about, picking up seeds and insects from the ground; growing thick climbers and tall herbaceous plants to give birds such as Wrens, which live half their lives on the ground, vital cover from predators.

*r: Dunnock* ♀

# WRENS

Wrens might be small and a somewhat nondescript brown but there's a reason they have their own pet name of 'Jenny Wren' – because they have such huge personalities. What the Wren lacks in size – it weighs only 9 grams (5/16 ounces) – it makes up for in character. Its huge voice is incredible for such a small bird, defending its territory vocally both loudly and frequently. You often hear a Wren long before you spot it. It's one of those birds that is great company for gardeners as it sings even through the winter months, which gives rise to its USA name of Winter Wren.

Spotting 'your' Wren isn't easy as they creep about keeping to the sidelines, but they are identifiable by their cocked tail, which is unlike that of any other bird. It's best to keep your eyes open early or late in the day: they favour dusk for hopping about, often on the ground, from one bit of cover to another and they'll often have a regular 'track' that they follow from shrub to pot plant and so on.

The Wren's nesting habits are quite remarkable. The male can build some six or seven nests in a year, often in outlandish places such as the pocket of an old coat hung up in the shed. In fact, unused sheds are favourite places and my old shed has been home to several generations of Wren. It's great to see the fledglings' fluffy bottoms pressed against the window as they learn to fly, launching themselves from the window ledge to the old mower handle. Once built, the array of ball-like nests of woven grass and moss is thoroughly inspected by the female and she then lines the best nest with hair and feathers. The first brood is born in the spring and then the pair can nest again, with the fledged first brood helping to feed the second. I have seen this in action: the tiny, but fully fledged chicks busily bringing tasty morsels such as insects, spiders and small snails back for a second brood. But what about those spare nests? They don't go to waste as the industrious male Wren quite often has up to three females inhabiting his nests each year.

CHAPTER TWO

# INTERESTING FACTS ABOUT BIRDS

# INTERESTING FACTS ABOUT BIRDS

**1** ## THE FASTEST BIRD ON EARTH IS...

…the Peregrine Falcon. When it's hunting, it makes spectacular dives or 'stoops', reaching recorded airspeeds of up to 242 mph (389 km/h). But the fastest bird when flying on the level is the Swift and this zippy flyer has hit a top recorded airspeed of 105 mph (169 km/h).

**2** ## OWLS CANNOT MOVE THEIR EYES

Owls' eyeballs are tubular in shape and they can rotate their head 270°, which is further than any other animal and allows them to achieve 360° vision. Many Owls hunt at night and so also have exceptional hearing while some, such as Barn Owls, have asymmetric ear openings so they can pinpoint their prey more accurately.

**3** ## BIRDS CAN SPEND A LOT OF TIME FLYING

The Albatross is the largest living flying bird and flies up to 600 miles (965 km) in one day. In its lifetime, an Albatross will cover around 15 million miles (24 million km) – the equivalent of flying to the moon and back 18 times! When the young Albatross leaves the nest for the first time, it will spend at least seven years flying out at sea before it returns to land. During that maiden flight, a typical Albatross will cover something close to 1.5 million miles (2.4 million km). More common birds can also spend a great deal of time on the wing. A Swallow spends the first four years of its life in the air, while the Swift spends 10 months of each year in flight.

*l: Swallows ♂ ♀*

## 4 BIRDS ORIGINALLY EVOLVED FROM DINOSAURS

Fossil evidence shows that birds shared characteristic features with dinosaurs such as hollow bones, nest building and brooding behaviour. Some of these weren't flying dinosaurs, but their remains show they had fully formed feathers closely resembling those of birds. Perhaps the closest relation is Archaeopteryx, which lived approximately 147 million years ago, but this 'bird' had a long bony tail and teeth, as well as wings.

## 5 THE ONLY KNOWN POISONOUS BIRD IN THE WORLD IS...

...the Hooded Pitohui of the island of New Guinea. The poison is found in its skin and feathers.

## 6 PIGEONS WERE RADIOS IN THE WORLD WARS

With man-made communication methods unreliable and basic at the time, it fell to the humble pigeon to transport thousands of messages from the battle lines at the Front. Over 300,000 pigeons were used during both World Wars, with 32 awarded The Dickin Medal – the animal world's Victoria Cross. Pigeons can also recognize human faces and, apparently, even learn to read. Scientists have established that pigeons can be taught to recognize around 50 words and, crucially, can distinguish words from non-words.

## 7 CROWS AND RAVENS ARE EXTREMELY INTELLIGENT

Crows can use tools and solve logic puzzles while scientists believe that Ravens may even pre-plan their tasks – a trait previously thought to be exclusively human. Crows are also very good at learning adaptive behaviour; they're known to memorize the routes of bin lorries so they can get some tasty snacks.

## 8   SOME BIRD SPECIES MIGRATE LONG DISTANCES

Across the world around 4,000 bird species are migratory, which is around 40%. In the UK, around half of bird species migrate, whether that means leaving the country to winter in warmer climates or leaving colder climates such as Scandinavia to winter in the UK. In North America, 350 bird species migrate, about 27% of the total number. Some birds also migrate by altitude; they breed in upland areas in the summer and head to lowland areas for the winter.

## 9   STARLINGS CAN MIMIC

As well as good songbirds, Starlings are brilliant mimics and can copy the songs other birds make. They can also mimic the calls of frogs and various mammals, and even mechanical noises such as a car revving.

## 10   SOME BIRDS COVER THEMSELVES IN ANTS

Cardinals, Jays and Blackbirds, along with several other bird species, sometimes cover themselves in crushed or living ants, smearing them over their feathers, or allowing them to crawl over their bodies. Scientists still aren't sure what the purpose of 'anting' is, but it's believed that the birds use the formic acid secreted by the ants during their 'ant bath' to help get rid of lice and other parasites.

# PIGEONS, WOOD PIGEONS AND COLLARED DOVES

Regarded as a pest by many, the Feral Pigeon is the result of us breeding it centuries ago for both sport and food. The ancient dovecotes you see in old buildings were once home to hundreds of 'squabs' – young pigeons –which were a staple part of the diet in olden times. Pigeons are extremely variable to look at, ranging from mottled white through to browns, greys and almost black – but grey is the main theme. They're also successful breeders, raising several broods each season, as well as absolute eating machines – I've watched a Pigeon sit in a redcurrant bush, its weight bending the branches to breaking point, systematically plucking each fruit until the bush was bare. But it's too unkind to dismiss these birds as simple pests, especially when homing and racing pigeons have been around since ancient times and 'Pigeon Posts' have existed all over the world, even up to the present day.

Wood Pigeons are very similar: larger if anything, and with a rosy breast, white collar and white bars on the wings. They're shyer than the Feral Pigeon but still a common sight in the garden.

I have a soft spot for Collared Doves, with their gentle cooing call and habit of sticking together in their pairs as they feed and fly about. They're easy to tell apart from Pigeons, as their plumage is a pale, warm buff colour with that distinctive black collar. Although their call might seem like the soundtrack to summer, Collared Doves were only sighted in the UK for the first time in 1952 – since then the number of breeding pairs has grown to something like 1 million.

*r: Collared Doves, Wood Pigeons*

CHAPTER THREE

# HABITAT
# ESSENTIALS

W hile birds live in all sorts of wildly diverse places, ranging from mountains and forests to huge deserts and tiny islands in vast oceans, many birds never leave their local habitats, spending their lives within a few square miles. Some do migrate to warmer countries when the weather changes and some of these migrations can be tens of thousands of miles long, but they return to the same places year after year. It's easy to forget just how far that little Swallow has travelled in its lifetime when you're watching it darting about, catching insects on the wing.

The great thing is that you don't need to go far to find birds. Just look out of the window and you'll see some. Stand at the bus stop or in the park and just look up – they're all around you and we take them for granted. That means your garden, however small, is a potential home and habitat for any number of them, especially if you set about making it more bird friendly. It's well worth doing because, although only around 30 species of birds are regular visitors to UK gardens, more than 140 species have been recorded, so you never quite know what might suddenly appear feeding on your Holly berries. Across the Atlantic, the regular visitors you get depends very much on where you live, but it's fair to say there are around 1,000 bird species that occasionally drop in to backyards in the USA.

But it doesn't really matter where in the world you're gardening, because birds all want essentially the same things from their home habitat: the key ingredients that make them feel safe and secure. These can all easily be provided in the average garden. In fact, you'll be amazed just how much you can do to make even a small garden welcoming and inviting for a wide range of birds.

*r: Song Thrush* ♀

Planting with birds in mind is vital for a few fundamental reasons. Plants and birds are wonderfully intertwined, with many plants offering birds exactly the type of shelter they need to rest, roost, nest and mate. The twiggy shelter that plants provide also offers birds the best protection from predators – other than simply flying away. Then there's the plain fact that plants are also an ever-giving larder for all sorts of birds, whether that's seeds, berries or insects, or in the case of predatory birds, other birds and their eggs. Chances are that you already have some great plants in your garden but there's always room for more, isn't there? That's when you need to make the right choices and start thinking like a bird, choosing things that will make your garden a haven all year round, rich in foodstuffs such as berries, seeds and insects.

# BALCONIES AND WINDOWSILLS

Making the most of your space can be as simple as adding a hanging basket, a window box and a few feeders. Even these tiny spaces can be brilliant for birds, especially as they're at sky level, making perfect rest and feed stops for birds. You'll have room for more flowers and plants than you might think, perhaps even a tree in a pot. The more plants you have, the more they will create a habitat and the more bird friendly your balcony or windowsill will be.

# SUBURBAN GARDENS

These larger gardens often have mature trees and shrubs and can become home to many different resident birds, each with their own territory. But there's also plenty of scope to add in more bird-friendly features, whether that's a cluster of berrying shrubs or a swathe of flowering annuals and meadow plants. Plant a border of seed-bearing perennials and grasses that you can leave standing as a winter feature – not only will they look fantastic but they'll also provide seeds, insects and cover for the birds through the harshest months. Make sure you have some plants close to the house to attract the birds to where you can see them.

# SMALL GARDENS

Small gardens are often some of the best spaces for birds – especially as they often back on to or run alongside other gardens, which gives the birds a brilliant 'green corridor' to flit from one garden to another. There is an enormous amount you can do to attract birds, such as planting a small tree or a cluster of shrubs for shelter and berries. Think about making a garden pond or a bog garden, which are brilliant for providing essential water for drinking and bathing but also attract insects for birds to feed on.

# THINK LIKE A BIRD

*The key ingredients a bird needs from your garden
are essentially very simple:*

**SHELTER** is vital to make birds feel safe in your garden. Good
shelter offers them the security to roost and rest, check their
feathers and preen in safety, which is vital to their health. Good
shelter also offers safe and sturdy places for them to nest and
bring up their young. Shelter mainly comes from trees and
shrubs, but climbers such as honeysuckle and clematis trained
up trelliswork can offer brilliant nesting spots and of course
you can always add your own nest boxes to help matters along.

**FOOD** supply is crucial for birds. They eat regularly and your
garden can provide a great deal of what they need. Of course,
you can put out feeders and perhaps build a bird table, but the
garden itself needs to be a constant supply of food in its own
right. Planting shrubs, trees and climbers that produce plenty
of berries is a good start, but many birds are seed eaters and
these are easily supplied by growing lots of seed-bearing annuals
and leaving seed heads on herbaceous plants in late summer
and autumn for the birds to feed on as food becomes scarcer.
Leaving those stems will also help the insect-eating birds
because, where you have plants – even if they're fading – you
will have insects feeding on the plant matter or other insects.

**WATER** in some shape or form – a pond, a birdbath or even
just a saucer on the bird table – is a good idea. Birds need
to drink and also to wash their feathers to keep them in top
condition. They can do that in other gardens or even in
puddles but really you want to see them doing it in your
garden, especially as it takes a while for them to have a good
wash, giving you a chance to observe and enjoy their antics.

*r: Wren* ♀

# SPARROWS AND DUNNOCKS

These little birds are some of the most common species you're likely to get visiting your garden. You've probably barely noticed them, with their nondescript plumage in dull browns and greys, yet they're bound to live in your backyard and neighbourhood.

House Sparrows have lived alongside us for thousands of years, scavenging seed from the very first farmers to settle the land. They like to nest in colonies, with their chirpy chatter and gregarious ways. They also like to congregate in groups but are swift to scatter should they be surprised by the back door or the garden gate opening. But that moment before they scatter is what I especially love about these little birds – they are incredibly sociable, gathering in twittering little groups in a bramble bush or on the bird table to feed. They remind me of gangs of school children in the playground, huddled in their little group, chattering and bickering.

Tree sparrows are similar in looks but generally shyer and more likely to be seen in rural areas. Sadly, both these birds are in decline, probably as a result of modern farming practices and insecticide use, which makes garden habitats and feeders even more important.

Dunnocks, or Hedge Sparrows as they're also known, are small and greyish brown and you'll often spot them scrimping for insects at the bottom of a hedge or shrubs. Like House Sparrows they eat insects, as well as seeds and berries in the

*r: House Sparrows ♂*

winter months. Their nests are tucked away in dense vegetation such as shrubs or hedges, often up to 1.5 metres (5 feet) above the ground, and you tend to spot them on their own or perhaps with one or two others – not in the great chattering groups like the House Sparrow. But their quiet ways belie an adventurous sex life, with males and females often breeding with several different partners throughout the season.

CHAPTER FOUR

# LAYERED
# PLANTING

You might think that your garden isn't one that birds would be especially interested in – most just fly overhead and don't particularly drop in, except the pigeons. But all gardens are a potential habitat for birds and there are simple techniques for managing and planning them that really boost their attractiveness to birds. Take a step back and analyse your garden and what it already has to offer – you'll be surprised. The key thing is layered planting, which is exactly what it sounds like: planting from top to bottom in stages. Birds need certain conditions to encourage them to visit or take up residence in your garden and layered planting allows them to move freely from one safe space to another.

## WHAT'S IN THE LAYERS?

Layered planting makes your garden three-dimensional. So instead of just considering it from front to back, think about it from top to bottom. The top layer is the trees, or tree if you have a small garden. You might even be 'borrowing' a tree from a neighbouring garden. Even a single tree is hugely important for birds, although a group is even better. Trees provide height and cover to allow birds such as Hawks and Woodpeckers to swoop down and pick up insects and larger prey.

The next layer is the shrubs and climbers – the understorey of dense twiggy things that birds can use for shelter all year round. The idea is to create something like the natural edge that you get to a patch of woodland, with differences in height to create layers for the birds to perch in, secure and sheltered from predators by twigs and foliage. Blue Tits, for example, flit from shrub to shrub, using them almost as stepping stones.

*l: Blue Tit, Great Spotted Woodpecker*

Hedges play a huge part in the garden ecosystem at this middle layer; especially mature ones that have been allowed to fruit. Thick hedgerows also provide fantastic shelter for birds, particularly during the nesting season, so it's vital to confine hedge trimming to the winter months and ideally, refrain from trimming the whole hedge, allowing some fruiting and wayward growth.

The bottom layer is the lower general planting that makes up much of our gardens: annuals, perennials and the lawn, of course. This is where you can make a lot of impact in no time at all, mainly by doing nothing. Simply letting the plants go to seed and leaving some areas of long uncut grass creates a haven for insects, which will provide food for many birds.

Layered planting encourages a varied ecosystem to evolve, drawing in bees, butterflies, moths and hoverflies, which will not only provide food for the birds but also plenty of additional wildlife for you to look at.

# PLANNING AND PLANTING

There is a simple formula to planning a space and that is to have layered planting around the edges with an area of open space – either lawn or patio – in the middle. This works whatever the size of your garden, even if it's a courtyard garden or balcony and you're growing everything in pots.

Boundaries are the perfect places for bird habitats, especially if your neighbours are keen gardeners too. If you can, plant a hedge or a mixture of flowering and fruiting shrubs to give the birds brilliant shelter and nesting spaces. If you have fences or walls, then grow climbers such as Honeysuckle and Wisteria or train shrubs like Firethorn on them. Wall-trained fruit trees are also a good option.

Trees are one of the best resources for birds, giving them shelter, good perches and keeping them safely above ground predators like your neighbour's cat. Even the smallest garden has space for a tree and you'll be surprised how many trees an average garden will support without looking overgrown. They key is choosing the right variety so it won't outgrow its space, so read the label carefully and look at trees in neighbouring parks and gardens for ideas. Growing trees in pots is a brilliant option if you're hesitant or very short of space.

Herbaceous plants fill in that middle ground between the tree and shrub layer and that all-important open space. There are so many brilliant herbaceous plants to choose from, able to suit all soils, sun or shade. Look for single flowers, which will attract the maximum number of insects – and the birds that prey on them. Anything that produces copious seeds is also a plus for seed-eating birds, while ornamental grasses provide excellent shelter and good nesting material.

Lawn might not seem like a great habitat but let the wildflowers like Clover and Selfheal flower and it will be abuzz with insects attracting many birds.

Long grass or meadow is a wonderful addition to the garden and it's worth dedicating a spot specifically for this. You can either just let the grass grow or clear the ground and plant one of the flowering meadow mixes specifically formulated to attract birds.

## WHICH PLANTS WILL SUIT MY GARDEN?

Everyone's garden is different – some are sunny, while others are shady, dry, damp or more likely a mixture – and that will dictate the plants you can grow to some degree. Which direction your garden faces is very important, especially in the winter when the sun is low. For instance, a north-facing garden in winter is almost completely shaded and so gets and stays very cold, whereas a south-facing one will nearly always get some sun and is generally warmer, so you can grow more sun-loving, slightly tender plants such as Lavenders. If there are buildings or trees that overshadow your garden, you'll need more shade-loving plants – although many trees allow some light through in a sort of dappled shade. Ideally, you need to know these things about your garden before you start spending money on plants.

# CHOOSING PLANTS

There are so many plants to choose from – many of them great for birds – that it's hard to know where to start. Don't get carried away just because you like the look of something: take care to pick the right size plant for your garden. You don't want to plant something that's going to romp away and take over your border or a tree that will become a problem in a few years. The average garden simply does not have room for an oak tree, unless it's in a pot. Having said that, don't limit your choices too much – it's surprising just how many different plants can comfortably fit into even a small garden. Remember birds like lots of different plants, so the more the merrier.

Choose plants that flower and fruit in different seasons if you can – the lists in Chapters 5, 6, 7 and 8 will help you – so your garden has something to offer in all seasons. Remember that many birds eat insects and they will be attracted to flowering plants all year round, but especially in spring and summer, which is when birds need plenty of easily found insects to feed their chicks.

Read the label carefully before you buy – you don't want to waste money, time and effort planting something that isn't going to thrive.

## UNDERSTANDING THE LABEL

*When it comes to choosing plants pay special attention to the label – it will have just about everything you need to know on it in symbols or as a description.*

NAME: The label front usually has a picture of the plant, plus its common name and its Latin name to avoid any confusion.

MATURE SIZE AND SHAPE: Sometimes this is a symbol showing the shape of the plant and its overall size after several years.

DESCRIPTION: This lets you know what sort of plant it is – perennial, tree and so on – as well as any special features it may have, such as autumn colour, and the main season of interest, which is often when it flowers, but not always.

LIGHT REQUIREMENTS: How much sun the plant needs to thrive is often shown as a symbol of a full sun, half sun or shaded sun. Either that or there's a super-short description, but this is one of the most crucial things to be aware of. Here's what the symbols mean:

**Full sun** – the plant needs at least six hours of sunlight a day.

**Part shade** – around three hours of sunlight a day.

**Full shade** – ideally this needs to be shaded from the sun at all times, but it can often cope with dappled shade as long as it doesn't get too exposed.

WATERING: A symbol of some drops often indicates how much water the plant needs. Sometimes it's mentioned in the plant description, such as 'requires moisture retentive soil' or, more simply, 'water weekly'.

HARDINESS: This is nearly always shown by a symbol that indicates the minimum winter temperature the plant can survive. Often it's also marked in USDA Hardiness Zones. Because the USA is so huge and has such a wild geographical area, the United States Department of Agriculture (USDA) developed a system to roughly categorize 13 zones by their minimum temperature.

*r: Culinary Herbs*

# BLACKBIRDS

However small your garden, you're bound to have a resident Blackbird. Blackbirds tend to be cautious birds, scuttling out from cover to feed on insects on the patio or scratching around beneath the shrubs. They'll sit tight, roosting in the shrubbery all winter, but once the days start to lengthen they fill the air with their liquid song – which is so beautiful that it's no wonder The Beatles wrote a homage to it. The singing often starts early in the season – and early in the day – and it mainly serves to mark its territory. Spotting the male Blackbird is easy – he's a beauty with his golden beak and glossy black feathers – while the female is a dull brown and can be mistaken for the Song Thrush, which it is related to. Pairs often start nesting early, producing a few broods each season, and tend to stay together for life, usually about three or four years. Blackbirds mainly feed on the ground, rootling through the leaf litter looking for insects and sometimes pulling up earthworms, but they'll also eat seeds and berries. I mostly see my resident Blackbird either singing from the apex of the shed roof or scuffling about under my Cherry tree. He's easily startled, squawking his alarm as he dashes back under cover, but his song is a joy.

# THRUSHES

Thrushes are some of the most common garden birds and the name encompasses a huge group, which share similar characteristics. The most often-seen member of this family is the Blackbird, but you'll certainly have heard the beautiful fluting song of the Song Thrush or its slightly larger cousin, the Mistle Thrush – although spotting them is more difficult with their excellent camouflage of speckled breasts and brown topsides. Thrushes are all fundamentally tree dwellers, but often come down to the ground to catch invertebrates or, in autumn, to gather berries. Berries are a big thing with Thrushes; in fact, the Mistle Thrush is named after its penchant for Mistletoe, which it does a brilliant job of propagating around the countryside. The bird scrapes its beak against a branch to remove the sticky berry goo, depositing the Mistletoe seed where it can take root on its host plant.

Other Thrushes are more commonly seen in winter, such as the large and brightly speckled Fieldfare and the much smaller Redwing. As autumn settles in, you might see either of these sweeping overhead in a great cloud. They've travelled to the UK from Iceland and Scandinavia, descending on berry trees and bushes – like my Holly tree – which they strip bare within a day or two before moving on. You'll see Fieldfares and Redwings in the USA too, as well as other members of the Thrush family that are firm garden favourites, such as Bluebirds and American Robins.

*l: Blackbirds ♂ ♀*

CHAPTER FIVE

# SPRING BIRDS AND PLANTS

Lying in bed in spring, listening to the riot of birdsong outside my window, is how I started to get interested in birds. There's simply no doubting when spring is on its way, as the birds well and truly proclaim it. Even in my suburban street, the garden comes loudly and vividly alive with the songs of birds in the spring. Every morning for weeks the dawn chorus wakes me up as the birds try to out-sing one another, all competing for mates and territory with every fibre of their being. They might not be the most exotic of birds but I can happily forgive the early start and share the sheer joy of spring as I listen to the liquid song of a Blackbird. In fact, because the 'Dawn Chorus' is such a regular phenomenon across the world, there's even an International Dawn Chorus Day on the first Sunday in May each year, which encourages people to get up early to listen to birdsong.

The birds are especially lively because spring is the season for mating and, of course, nesting, which makes it a great time to spot different species, as well as to offer them a home in your garden. Get busy placing nesting boxes for resident birds if you haven't already. Don't trim your hedges or prune trees in case you disturb nesting birds – you want them to feel safe and at home, especially as some birds such as Blue Tits will nest in the same place year after year. Robins and Wrens love nesting in sheds and outhouses, so leave a pane of glass out of the window or some space on a shelf.

*r: Wren ♂*

# SPRING BIRDS YOU'RE LIKELY TO SEE

Resident birds such as Tits, Finches, Thrushes and Sparrows are busy feeding broods of chicks and will use feeders regularly.

Summer visitors start to arrive as the season progresses, including migrants from Africa such as Swallows, House Martins and Swifts, which you'll see darting about in the evenings catching insects.

You might hear the distinctive call of the Cuckoo too – though don't mistake it for the 'coo-coo' of the Collared Dove.

Goldfinches reach their peak numbers in many gardens in late spring. These returning migrants pass through en masse in what is called, rather beautifully, 'a charm'. They rely on garden plants and feeders to keep them going at this time of year because there is probably little food available in the countryside.

## THINGS TO DO

• Put out food for busy parent birds with hungry mouths to feed. You might want to use 'summer' food mixes as spring progresses, which contain things like Sunflower seed kernels to boost energy.

• Make sure there is water at hand for bathing and drinking as the weather gets warmer. Keep your water dish and birdbath freshly topped up and clean – hygiene is hugely important to prevent disease.

*r: Goldfinch ♂*

• It's easy to grow some quick flowering annuals, even in the smallest space. These will attract insects into the garden as well as providing seeds later for seed-eating birds. Many flowers, such as Cornflowers, Pot Marigolds and Love-in-a-Mist, are super-easy to grow and look great in the garden too.

• It's difficult for a gardener to embrace weeds and their seeds but some birds absolutely thrive on them, especially Goldfinches, which love Dandelion, Teasel and Thistle seeds. So don't be afraid to let the weeds grow or, if you can't bear it, simply plant a Teasel or two – they'll look great in the border.

# GARDEN PLANTS FOR SPRING

TREES, SHRUBS AND CLIMBERS

## HAWTHORN
*Crataegus species*

There are few trees or shrubs that are better for wildlife
than the Hawthorn. Plant it as part of a hedge, as
a shrub or choose a variety to grow as a tree.

**Good for:** Spring blossom and autumn fruits. Can be
trimmed as a hedge, pruned into shape as a shrub or
trained as a tree. Makes a brilliantly dense, twiggy
cover for nesting and roosting birds.

**Garden merit:** The lovely late spring flowers of native
species are followed by red fruits that often last into
late autumn and early winter, when they provide a very
welcome meal for the birds. *Crataegus schraderiana*
makes a highly ornamental feature tree with its large
red fruits, while *Crataegus laevigata* 'Paul's Scarlet'
has rich pink-red double flowers.

## CHERRY
*Prunus species*

Cherries are beautiful garden trees and they come in
all shapes and sizes, so there's a variety that will suit
even the smallest of gardens. As well as fruiting
Cherries for the kitchen garden and dwarf weeping
varieties, there are the Japanese forms with wonderful
blossom in the spring.

**Good for:** The aptly named Bird Cherry, *Prunus padus*, is probably the best variety for birds although it's better suited to larger gardens. But even many of the ornamental flowering Cherries bear small, sour fruits that the birds will happily eat.

**Garden merit:** The Yoshino Cherry, *Prunus x yedoensis*, is a beautiful early flowering variety with a great deal of charm. Small enough for patio pots, the dwarf variety *Prunus incisa* 'Kojo-no-mai' has masses of blossom.

## ELDER
*Sambucus species*

Shrubby Elders are so easy to grow and will suit most garden soils, looking good in the border with other plants or as part of a boundary planting.

**Good for:** Spring blossom, which attracts a great many insects, followed by a profusion of berries in late summer. Robins, Waxwings and Orioles are all fans of the fruit, among many others.

**Garden merit:** There are some great garden choices, such as *Sambucus nigra* 'Black Lace' with finely cut purple leaves, and I love *Sambucus nigra* 'Black Beauty', with dark leaves and candyfloss-pink flowers in spring.

*r: Cherry*

## DOGWOOD

*Cornus species*

There are so many great Dogwood
varieties to choose from, some of them
native too. Many are grown for winter
interest in the garden, but the spring
flowering varieties make a great feature
plant. Remember it's the fruit that will
interest the birds, so if you're growing
them for coloured stems, don't cut them
back every year.

**Good for:** Spring flowers attract some
insects, but it's the late fruit that is
the main attraction for birds. Shrubby
growth provides good shelter too.

**Garden merit:** Many of the beautiful
flowering species, such as *Cornus nutallii* and *Cornus
florida*, bear lots of fruit, attracting many species of
birds. These are slow-growing large shrubs or small
trees, such as the Cornelian Cherry *Cornus mas*, while
the coloured stem *Cornus alba* is an easy-to-grow shrub
that will suit most gardens.

## SNOWY MESPILUS/SERVICEBERRY

*Amelanchier species*

A super tree or multi-stem shrub that is great for the
smaller garden, this beautiful plant has a froth of spring
blossom followed by masses of cherry-like fruits in
summer and then glorious autumn colour.

*r: Dogwood*

**Good for:** Provides perches and cover for birds in addition to summer fruits. Attracts Robins, Waxwings, Cardinals and many other songbirds.

**Garden merit:** A feature plant for the small garden with all-year-round interest. Even in winter the bare stems make an airy silhouette that looks great set against evergreen foliage or a dark hedge or fence.

## GUELDER ROSE
*Viburnum species*

It's not hard to find an attractive species of Viburnum and many of them are brilliant for birds with their spring flowers and autumn fruits.

**Good for:** The showy spring flowers are excellent for attracting insects that birds will feed on, but it's the bunches of glossy fruits that pull in birds like Bullfinches, Waxwings, Mistle Thrushes and Jays in the autumn. All Viburnums make excellent shelter and cover for birds.

**Garden merit:** The Guelder Rose is one of the best for both birds and garden but it can be a big shrub. *Viburnum opulus* 'Compactum' stays a manageable size and, as well as producing berries, its leaves colour beautifully in autumn. Other species of Viburnum are also excellent for garden planting, such as *Viburnum tinus*, which flowers in late winter and early spring followed by clusters of black berries. *Viburnum plicatum* has flattened frothy heads of flowers followed by berries.

## WISTERIA
*Wisteria species*

A highly ornamental and vigorous-growing climber, Wisteria makes a great addition to most gardens for its beautiful, often fragrant, flowers and elegant, leafy growth habit.

**Good for:** The masses of long racemes of flowers in spring are good for attracting insects that birds such as Flycatchers and Warblers will feed on. The twining leafy growth is superb for birds to shelter and nest in.

**Garden merit:** Wisteria is a beautiful, non-clinging climber to train against house or garden walls, fences and pergolas. You can even train it to grow as a free-standing umbrella shape, with some support and severe pruning. Choose *Wisteria sinensis* varieties for fragrant flowers before the leaves. *Wisteria floribunda* flowers are often later and larger but less scented.

## LAWN FLOWERS – DAISY, CLOVER, DANDELION

*Bellis, Trifolium and Taraxacum species*

A simple area of lawn left untreated with chemicals and dotted with wildflowers is a huge boon to birds. Leave some areas to grow long and wild, and mow others to make space for sitting or games, while still allowing flowers to bloom.

**Good for:** All sorts of birds love scratching about in a lawn or long grass, looking for insects, invertebrates and seeds. Expect to see Blackbirds, Sparrows and Finches, as well as larger birds such as Jays and Woodpeckers, attracted by the insects in the lawn.

**Garden merit:** An untreated, untamed lawn is a kaleidoscope of small flowers and plants as well as grass. It's a far cry from a formal lawn of uniform, green grass and adds an extra dimension of interest to the garden. Many plants such as Clover also cope with drought better than grass, meaning your 'lawn' will look healthier through the summer months.

## EVENING PRIMROSE
*Oenethera species*

Native to the USA, the 'wild' Evening
Primrose has been naturalized in the
UK for centuries. Most varieties have
clear yellow flowers that appear in
late spring and early summer and
are brilliant for wildlife.

**Good for:** The flowers attract many
moths and other insects, pulling
in insect-eating birds, while the
seeds are favourites of birds such
as Greenfinches and Siskins.

**Garden merit:** Evening Primrose
comes in many forms, some short-
lived with others more perennial.
All prefer well-drained, dry conditions and look
great self-seeding around a gravel garden. The
common variety is *Oenethera biennis*, an annual
or biennial bloomer, while *Oenethera speciosa* from
Mexico has delicate pink flowers. A favourite of
mine is *Oenethera missouriensis*, a perennial with
a low-growing, trailing habit.

## COW PARSLEY
*Anthriscus sylvestris*

Frothy white flowers and ferny foliage make
Queen Anne's Lace or Cow Parsley a favourite
for the wild garden.

*r: Evening Primrose*

**Good for:** The open flowers attract all sorts of insects, including soldier beetles, but it's the seeds later in the season that birds such as Sparrows love.

**Garden merit:** Cow Parsley looks great in a wild garden, border or running wild under trees. Its roots are also brilliant for absorbing heavy rainfall in spring so it's a useful plant for a poorly drained spot in the garden. Be warned, though: it is a vigorous self-seeder so make sure it doesn't take over your garden. There is an ornamental form, 'Ravenswing', with dark leaves, but it will mix and become diluted with the wild Cow Parsley.

## FALSE INDIGO
*Baptisia species*

With some species native to the USA, this perennial plant produces pea-like flowers, usually in clear shades of blue, in late spring and early summer.

**Good for:** The flowers are followed by eye-catching pods of seeds that rattle in the breeze as they dry out and birds such as Chickadees love.

**Garden merit:** Baptisia needs a well-drained soil and full sunshine to thrive. Plant it in the border with other sun-loving perennials such as Rudbeckia (Black-eyed Susan), where its blue-green foliage and large seedpods continue to give interest long after the flowers have faded.

*r: Cow Parsley*

# NESTING SPOTS AND BOXES

Spring is all about mating and nesting and the natural places to nest are usually trees, shrubs and hedges. Providing these plants helps to attract birds to settle down and raise their young in your garden, but nesting boxes can also offer safety and security and can be strategically placed to let you keep an eye on activity. The nesting season can last a long time – throughout the spring and even into the summer, with some birds such as Wood Pigeons having several broods of chicks. Dense trees, shrubs, climbers and hedges are perfect places for birds such as Dunnocks, Blackbirds and Robins to nest and even those thick conifer hedges that everyone loves to hate make brilliant nesting sites for Greenfinches and Goldcrests, as well as sometimes larger birds such as Crows or even Sparrowhawks.

## QUICK TIPS

It's a great time to make a nesting ball from twigs and wool to hang somewhere you can keep an eye on it, in the hope that birds will flock to it to pick out their favourite nesting materials. Use fabric, twine, wool, dead leaves, grass – anything natural that will degrade over time – and bind them together with twine or bendy willow stems to create a dense ball that you can hang high in a tree or shrub. You could even pack an old kitchen whisk with material, which has its own ready-made hanger.

Avoid siting a nesting box where it gets direct sunshine during the hottest part of the day. Fix it securely, ideally somewhere shaded by foliage and facing the hole anywhere between north-east and south-east.

Open-fronted nest boxes are best for Robins and Pied Wagtails, while boxes with a hole are more suited to Blue and Great Tits or Sparrows – depending on the size of the hole. Steer clear of fancy designs; simple is best and it's easy enough to make a basic box yourself with a few DIY skills.

*r: House Sparrow ♀*

# WOODPECKERS

Spring really starts for me when I hear the unmistakable laughing call of the Green Woodpecker – that Kookaburra-type laugh that earned it its folk name of Yaffle. This particular bird has lived around my garden for years, nesting either with my neighbours or me. Sometimes I also hear its characteristic 'rat-tat-tat' drumming sound – although I've read that Green Woodpeckers rarely drum, my Woodpecker happily ignores this truth. I also spot it regularly on the lawn, stalking about looking lordly and large with its rich green coat and scarlet hat, but flying swiftly away if I get too close. It's feeding on the ants in the lawn – its main food. Green Woodpeckers have a barbed spike of a tongue, which is very long and coated in a sticky substance that traps the ants and draws them into the Woodpecker's mouth.

The Great and Lesser Spotted Woodpeckers are smaller and easily distinguished from the Green with their black-and-white colouring. Telling them apart is the tricky thing, although size is a giveaway. Add to that the fact that the Lesser Spotted is a very shy little bird while the Great Spotted is as bold as they come, regularly visiting bird feeders and tables, often scaring off smaller birds with its brash ways. When they're not raiding the feeders, these live mainly on the larvae of wood- and bark-boring insects.

There are quite a few species of Woodpecker throughout the world, with some 16 species scattered across the USA. But besides those hard heads and beaks, all Woodpeckers also have specially adapted feet, with two toes facing forwards and two backwards, which enable them to climb extremely well. They also use their tail, which has especially strong tail feathers, to prop themselves in position, so they can hold their body far

enough away to carve their way into the tree. Another thing: while Woodpeckers do hammer to get at grubs and larvae in trees, chances are that the classic drumming sound you're hearing is mainly a territorial call, rather than a Woodpecker getting its lunch.

*r: Green Woodpecker ♂*

CHAPTER SIX

# SUMMER BIRDS AND PLANTS

It might sound strange but summer is often the worst time for spotting birds, especially in an urban garden. That's because there is plentiful food available out in the fields and wild spaces. Think about it – even wasteland in the city is home to masses of flowering and seeding plants in the summer months, all alive with insects. Then there's also the fact that the days are so long, allowing plenty of time for feeding from sun-up to very late evening. It all gives the birds plenty of choices besides your garden, so don't lose heart if they seem to be a bit thin on the ground. But it doesn't mean there aren't birds to be spotted, though, and summer is often the time that the migrating birds arrive in force. Those brilliant darting flyers, the Swallows, Swifts and House Martins, can start arriving in late spring, but often bad weather can delay them, and so you'll only really start to notice them in early summer.

As the season wears on into high summer, activity in the garden quietens down – literally, as male birds no longer have to sing to defend their territory or attract a mate. Many songbirds also moult in high summer, shedding their old, worn-out feathers and growing fresh ones so they're ready for autumn and winter. That makes them vulnerable to predators, so they retreat to the twiggy cover of your garden hedges and shrubs, which makes your garden an important refuge. This is also the time when many of the smaller perennial and annual plants will be flowering at their peak, attracting pollinating insects, aphids and insect predators – all potential food for birds.

# SUMMER BIRDS YOU'RE LIKELY TO SEE

In early summer, Blue Tits and Great Tits are everywhere sweeping through the garden as a family, feeding and perching in shrubs and trees, before moving off to the next.

You're bound to see young Robins in the garden in summer, although they're initially hard to identify as they have a brown speckled chest rather than the red breast of the adults. They have the same bold, inquisitive nature though, and will follow you about while you're weeding.

If you're lucky, this is the time of year you might get the odd visit from a hunting Sparrowhawk, often preying on birds even bigger than itself. You may even see a Little Owl, perhaps a young bird looking for its own patch.

## THINGS TO DO

• In summer, birds need plenty of water: a dish of water, a bird-bath or a pond are all valuable sources of drinking and bathing water. A well-placed birdbath is a great place to watch birds in summer, but do make sure you keep it clean and topped up.

• Early flowering annuals and grasses are a rich source of food for seed-eating birds. If you didn't get around to sowing any in the spring, do it now – the plants may well flower and seed later in the summer or early autumn.

• The kitchen garden is a brilliant source of insects on herbs, fruit and vegetables – as long as you don't spray them, of course. Add to the pulling power by planting companion plants and flowering herbs such as Rosemary, Marjoram and Fennel.

# GARDEN PLANTS FOR SUMMER

TREES, SHRUBS AND CLIMBERS

## FRUIT TREES – APPLE, PEAR, PLUM
*Malus, Pyrus and Prunus species*

Many fruit trees are swathed in beautiful early blossom,
followed by luscious crops of edible fruits.

**Good for:** Flower-eating birds such as Bullfinches
are attracted by the blossom, as well as pollinating
insects, which in turn attract birds such as Tits to feed
on them. Later in summer and autumn the fruits and
windfalls will provide plenty of food for insects again,
and for birds such as Thrushes.

**Garden merit:** Most gardens have space for a fruit tree,
even if it's in a pot or trained against a wall. Top Apple
varieties include *Malus domestica* 'Fiesta', 'Katy' and
'Spartan'. Look out for dwarfing rootstocks such as
M27 that will keep the tree small. The same applies to
Plums and Pears, and there are also patio varieties that
are great for growing in pots.

## ROSES
*Rosa species*

There is a Rose to suit every garden, from tiny patio
Roses to huge rambling varieties that will grow up into
trees. Grow the single-flowered forms to attract the
maximum number of insects for the insect-eating birds,
and aim for species and varieties that produce hips, as

many birds, such as Fieldfares and Mistle Thrushes, will also eat those. Smaller birds such as Tits and Blackbirds will use the thorny cover of climbing species as shelter from predators.

**Good for:** The flowers and foliage attract insects while the hips feed larger birds such as Blackbirds and Fieldfares in autumn. Climbing roses also provide excellent cover.

**Garden merit:** Roses are a must-have plant for many gardeners. In the border, shrub Roses such as *Rosa moyesii* and *Rosa glauca* have vivid single flowers followed by colourful autumn hips, while ramblers like *Rosa* 'Paul's Himalayan Musk' will clothe a tree, providing dense cover, as well as insects and hips. Roses attract over 200 insect species, including aphids, which are an important food for many small birds.

## FRUIT BUSHES – REDCURRANT, BLACKCURRANT, BLACKBERRY, LOGANBERRY
*Ribes and Rubus species*

Redcurrants, Blackcurrants and rambling fruit, such as thornless Blackberries and Loganberries, are all great plants for the kitchen garden, plus they're attractive to birds.

**Good for:** Summer fruits, which many birds love, plus the insect life that is attracted by spring flowers and lush foliage. Don't net your fruit, though, as birds can get caught in the fine netting.

**Garden merit:** These are attractive and productive bushes for the kitchen garden. There are also several varieties of ornamental flowering currant such as *Ribes sanguineum* and 'White Icicle' with clusters of spring flowers followed by small fruits. These might be inedible to us, but they're a feast for birds.

## SPIREA
*Spiraea species*

There are few shrubs as pretty and as easy to grow as Spirea, also known as Meadowsweet. As well as laden with flowers, it's incredibly forgiving of soil and climate and requires little maintenance.

**Good for:** The fluffy summer flowers are brilliant for insects, while the dense, twiggy stems right to the base are great cover for small birds – especially ground-creepers such as Wrens and Blackbirds. Several moth caterpillars also feed on the foliage.

**Garden merit:** There's a spot in most gardens for a Spirea, which range from compact shrubs for patio containers to mid-sized border fillers such as *Spiraea* 'Goldflame' with its bright foliage and masses of pink flowers produced freely over the summer. For the larger garden and a wilder style of planting, the white garlands of the 'bridal wreath' *Spiraea* 'Arguta' make a marvellous early summer show.

## LAVENDER
*Lavendula species*

Lavender is a must-have for the garden on so many levels – for scent, for flowers, for bees and butterflies and also for birds.

**Good for:** Goldfinches will feed on the seeds while House Martins, Swifts and Swallows are drawn by the insect life on Lavender bushes. The stems and foliage also provide excellent nesting material.

**Garden merit:** A brilliantly versatile plant for planting alone or with other plants, Lavender looks great edging a traditional border or planted in a contemporary gravel garden. It has a long season of interest, evergreen foliage and you can choose from dwarf varieties such as *Lavendula* 'Imperial Gem' to much taller and blousy plants, such as the classic English *Lavendula* 'Hidcote'.

## HONEYSUCKLE
*Lonicera species*

One of the most useful and attractive garden climbers, Honeysuckle is a magnet for wildlife. There are also shrub varieties that provide excellent cover and fragrant winter flowers.

*l: Spirea*

**Good for:** Summer flowers attract many insects, followed by autumn fruits, which birds such as Bullfinches, Warblers and Thrushes love. Climbing Honeysuckle makes a good sheltering and potential nesting spot, especially for Thrushes.

**Garden merit:** There are hundreds of beautiful varieties, some evergreen, many scented; some are climbers while others are useful shrubs. Climbing varieties such as *Lonicera* 'Graham Thomas' can be trained on walls or fences but look best scrambling through a hedge or onto an arch where the loose, top-heavy growth is supported. Shrubby forms often produce their fragrant flowers in the winter months, attracting insects, and providing a lift to the winter garden.

## CLEMATIS
*Clematis species*

Clematis are a garden essential with their vibrant flowers in all sorts of colours. Some species of these versatile climbers start flowering in spring, while others flower in early summer, and still more provide interest as the summer fades.

**Good for:** Spring bloomers have dense, thick foliage that provides excellent cover for nesting and feeding birds. After flowering, they produce feathery seed-heads in summer and autumn that attract many birds, including Sparrows and Finches.

**Garden merit:** One of the most useful and attractive plants for gardens large and small. Grow the vigorous spring-flowering species such as *Clematis montana* and *Clematis alpina* to create a screen or disguise an ugly shed or garage, while the more delicate *Clematis viticella* varieties look wonderful threading through shrubs and trelliswork.

PERENNIALS AND ANNUALS

## SUNFLOWER
*Helianthus species*

One of the top plants for pollinators and birds, this easy-to-grow annual is a brilliant and fun addition to any garden.

**Good for:** Mainly for the fantastic heads of energy-rich seeds that will attract a whole host of birds, including Finches, Sparrows, Nuthatches, Tits, Chickadees and Cardinals. Make sure you opt for single forms that produce large heads of seeds, rather than double or multi-headed forms.

**Garden merit:** Brilliant for the kitchen garden to attract those all-important pollinators, as well as the insect-eating birds that will help to keep your crops healthy. Use the really tall varieties such as *Helianthus* 'Russian Giant' to screen an ugly fence, shed or wall. Alternatively, plant

*r: Sunflower*

some with other annuals such as Sweet Peas (*Lathyrus odoratus*) and Love-in-a-Mist (*Nigella*) to create an annual flower bed that will also feed the birds later.

## LOVE-IN-A-MIST
*Nigella species*

*Nigella* is a fantastic, easy-to-grow annual that looks great with its lacy, jewel-coloured flowers followed by puffy, crown-like seed pods. It also self-seeds freely around the garden and provides plenty of seeds for seed-eating birds.

**Good for:** This annual is so quick to flower and then set seed that it provides seedpods jampacked with seeds for smaller birds to enjoy all summer long.

**Garden merit:** There are few places in the garden that won't look even better for a handful of *Nigella* adding a splash of dainty colour. *Nigella damascena* is the best form for flowers, especially the clear blue *Nigella damascena* 'Miss Jekyll' or the pink, white and blue *Nigella damascena* 'Persian Jewels'. *Nigella sativa* is far less showy but still great for birds – and for us too, as it is better known as Kalonji or Black Cumin.

*r: Love-in-a-Mist*

## CORNFLOWER
*Centaurea species*

This easy-to-grow annual or perennial is quick to germinate and produces flowers from late spring into summer. The perennials flower for a long period while the annuals grow and flower swiftly.

**Good for:** As it flowers so readily, it's also quick to go to seed, which Sparrows, Buntings and Finches enjoy.

**Garden merit:** Perennial species make good additions to the flower border while native species are great for a wild, meadow-style area. If you keep re-sowing the annuals regularly, you'll have flowers all summer long. Use them to scatter in bare spots, or as part of an annual or cut flower bed. The classic Cornflower, *Centaurea cyanus* or 'Bachelor's Buttons', is a brilliant summer sky blue but there are also white forms and a rich burgundy form, *Centaurea cyanus* or 'Black Ball'.

## NASTURTIUM
*Tropaeolum majus*

Big-growing and bold in leaf and flower, Nasturtium is an easy-to-grow annual that is also a fantastic space filler for dull corners and empty spots in the garden.

**Good for:** Ground-feeding birds use the large leaves and trailing stems as cover, darting out to feed. Those lush leaves and soft stems are also attractive to aphids, which in turn attract hungry birds. They also play host to some of the 'cabbage' White butterflies – although many birds won't touch them, House Sparrows will eat them.

**Garden merit:** Nasturtium is a must-have for the kitchen garden, where a few plants make ideal companion planting to attract blackfly away from your beans and 'cabbage' White butterflies away from your brassicas. The big leaves and flowers are also edible and rather tasty, so make a good crop in their own right.

## THISTLES
*Cirsium, Carduus, Eryngium and Echinops species*

While some Thistles are regarded by gardeners as weeds, many of the perennial varieties are excellent border plants with great value for wildlife and birds.

**Good for:** Goldfinches adore Thistle seeds, and you sometimes see flocks of these beautiful birds moving through a patch of Thistles. Many bees, butterflies and birds are also drawn to the nectar-rich flowers.

**Garden merit:** The Globe Thistle is a statuesque border plant while Sea Holly, *Eryngium*, is smaller with surreal metallic spiky blooms. Use them to add drama to the border, as part of a mixed planting with Roses and Grasses. Leave the stems to stand into the autumn to allow the birds to reap the seeds and to give added structure to the fading garden.

## GOLDENROD
*Solidago species*

Vigorous and strong growing, this perennial is not a good plant for the smaller garden but is a brilliant choice for attracting birds where you have the space to accommodate it.

**Good for:** The long season of flowers attracts many insects and the birds that prey on them, while the autumnal seeds are attractive to Goldfinches, Greenfinches, Linnets and Siskins, as well as Northern Cardinals and Chickadees.

**Garden merit:** A great choice for the 'wild' garden where it can establish in large stands of tall, golden flowers that are freely produced from high summer into early autumn. This is a dramatic perennial that is incredibly tolerant of poor soil and is easy to grow.

*r: Goldenrod*

# WATER FOR BIRDS

One of the essentials of life, a safe, clean water source is every bit as important for birds as finding food and a secure place to nest. Birds need water both for drinking, hugely important in the hot droughty spells of summer, and for bathing, which is vital for keeping their feathers in tip-top condition.

Birds get a great deal of their water from the food they eat – just think of those juicy worms and insects. However, seed-eating birds like Finches and Sparrows need to drink more frequently. Most birds drink once or twice a day, usually early in the morning or late in the evening, because drinking is one of their most vulnerable times when predators such as cats, or perhaps a Sparrowhawk, could pick them off.

Bathing also takes place most days, again early or late, and is essential to keep plumage in good condition and free from parasites. It's great to watch a bird preening itself after a bath, running its beak through its feathers and drying off in the sun. Far from being just a summer and cosmetic activity, bathing can make all the difference as to whether a bird survives the winter. Well-maintained, clean feathers are infinitely better at keeping a bird warm during the tough days of winter than ill-kept, dirty ones.

## QUICK TIPS

Birdbaths should be sturdy with a gentle gradient from shallow to deeper to allow different-sized birds to drink and bathe. Make sure the surface isn't too smooth or the birds won't be able to grip.

Clean your birdbath regularly and top it up daily with fresh water. This is especially important in hot weather when bacteria can build up, swiftly spreading disease through visiting birds. Keep your birdbath free of ice in winter and top up with warm water from the kettle. It's so important to give birds a regular supply of water throughout the difficult winter months.
A well-designed garden pond also provides a safe water source for bathing and drinking, as well as attracting insects into the garden – a potential food source for birds.

*r: Long Tailed Tits ♂ ♀*

# SWIFTS, SWALLOWS AND HOUSE MARTINS

As spring begins to turn into summer, the arrival of the Swifts is unmistakable. The air is filled with groups of swooping birds, their shrieks and screams reverberating among the rooftops as they fly in from overseas. Swifts stay in the air for most of their lives, only landing to breed in the eaves of buildings. They even gather their nest-building elements, such as feathers, leaves and grass, while flying. But they're also the first to leave as summer starts to fade, heading for the warmer weather of Africa for the winter months.

Swallows make this extraordinary journey each spring and autumn, too. They gather in great chatty groups before nesting in barns, sheds and outhouses. Swallows have a great penchant for gathering on power lines, twittering sociably and volubly. Sometimes you'll see a single bird arrive and perch, twittering, and within minutes there will be dozens to see, easy to spot with their long tails outlined against the sky.

Like Swifts, House Martins build their nests under the eaves of houses but will also nest under bridges, building their cup-shaped homes from pellets of mud painstakingly cemented together in a similar fashion to those of Swallows'.

Telling these three common summer visitors apart isn't easy at first glance. They're all fundamentally similar in looks and behaviour but there are easy-to-spot differences. Swifts have a piercing call with scythe-like wings and a short forked tail. Swallows have deeply swept-back wings, a white tummy and

a long forked tail like no other, as is their habit of twittering on power lines. With their black-and-white plumage and forked tail, House Martins look similar to Swallows at first sight, but they're generally smaller and dumpier with a short forked tail and white face, tummy and a broad band of white across the back.

*from left to right: Swift, House Martin, Swallow*

CHAPTER SEVEN

# AUTUMN BIRDS AND PLANTS

Surprisingly, autumn provides some of the best opportunities for attracting birds into your garden, as the growing season draws to a close and the leaves start to turn. That's especially so when food becomes harder to find in the wider landscape – birds will start to get braver and hungrier, appearing in gardens regularly so you can get a really good look at them. That's when your garden can become a larder for the birds: your garden plants offer seeds and berries, and you can give a helping hand by stocking your bird table and feeders.

Autumn is a season of movement for many bird species, with birds such as House Martins heading for warmer winter quarters, and others such as Redwings and Fieldfares arriving, flocking through gardens in search of berries. While there are still plenty of seeds and insects around in the countryside, the number of birds migrating back for the winter is increasing and they will heartily appreciate a pit stop, wherever it is. My Holly tree has been a regular stop for a flock of Redwings for years and they will pick it clean of berries in a single day. You'll spot foraging flocks of all kinds, moving across the countryside in great sweeps in search of food. Keep your eyes open and you might catch them appearing in your garden, especially if there are plenty of berries and seeds on offer.

## AUTUMN BIRDS YOU'RE LIKELY TO SEE

Look out for flocks of dainty Goldcrests and sometimes Firecrests, especially in conifers, Holly or Yew trees. These are more likely to be spotted in autumn and winter, although you'll need to be keen-eyed as each bird is only the size of a coin.

Easier to spot are much larger Fieldfares and Redwings, as well as the beautiful but less common Waxwing. These Thrush-like birds love red berries of all types and will also feed on fallen fruit – a good reason to not tidy up your windfalls.

Keep your ears open for the characteristic 'twit-twoo' call of Tawny Owls marking their territory as the autumn progresses. At the other end of the size scale, Robins will also be vocal in advertising their ownership on a patch of garden, singing lustily and repeatedly as the days draw in.

## THINGS TO DO

• Autumn is a great time for getting on with gardening jobs as far as birds are concerned because you won't be disturbing nesting or mating. It's also a chance to clean out nestboxes and to put up new ones so birds have plenty of time to get familiar with them before they use them for their families.

• This is the perfect time to carry out shrub pruning and hedge trimming. Don't be too drastic, though, or you'll open up the plants too much for birds to want to nest in them the following spring. If possible, leave berrying shrubs alone until birds have picked them clean.

• If you're thinking about construction work, such as putting in a new pond, this is the time; not only will any disruption to birds be kept to a minimum, but the habitat will also have time to settle down over winter and new plants will establish and grow away next spring.

• Don't be too snip-happy with the secateurs. Leave stems of herbaceous plants such as Asters, Globe Thistle and Goldenrod as long as you can. Not only will birds have the seeds, but Wrens and Blackbirds will use the shelter the stems provide to move around the garden in search of insects.

• Keep the bird table topped up with fallen fruit and water, especially as the weather turns colder. Leaving fruit on the trees or on the ground will always attract hungry birds, too.

• As the autumn wears on and the weather gets colder, natural food resources will become scarcer and you'll notice birds getting braver and more territorial about your garden. As you spot the signs, you can start to increase the amount of foodand water you put out. Don't forget that those wintering birds such as Blackcaps will be appearing any minute now too.

*r: Redwing ♀*

# GARDEN PLANTS FOR AUTUMN

TREES, SHRUBS AND CLIMBERS

### ROWAN
*Sorbus species*

These beautifully
ornamental trees have
lovely foliage and are
perfect for smaller gardens,
but their main selling
point is the clusters of
brightly coloured fruits
in autumn that are a
favourite food of birds.

**Good for:** Those plentiful
fruits are fantastic food
for many birds, especially
Blackbirds, Thrushes,
Redwings and Waxwings.

**Garden merit:** You can't
beat a Rowan for beauty
and wildlife appeal.
Choose the native species
for maximum pulling factor for birds but all
species bear large juicy fruits, some in shades
of orange, yellow, pink or even white, and
providing much-needed sustenance for hungry
birds at some point during the winter months.

*r: Rowan*

## BEAUTYBERRY

*Callicarpa americana*

The Beautyberry is one of those plants that is intrinsically dull and unassuming for much of the year – until it drops its leaves in autumn, allowing the brilliantly coloured berries to suddenly demand centre stage in the garden.

**Good for:** In the USA, you can expect to see Robins, Cardinals, Mockingbirds and Towhees taking the fruit. In the UK, fruit-eating birds will often leave these brightly coloured berries until last, although they are a favourite of Blackcaps.

**Garden merit:** Plant one or more *Callicarpa* shrubs towards the back of a border and you won't regret it. Those shiny white or purple fruits might be small but they're packed onto the twiggy stems and shine out in the autumn garden, lasting for a good time before the birds get hungry enough to plunder them.

## COTONEASTER

*Cotoneaster species*

While Cotoneaster might seem a little 'ordinary', it's a top gardener performer – as well as a great choice for the bird-friendly habitat.

**Good for:** Fieldfares, Redwings and Waxwings love the fruits, while many smaller birds appreciate the dense twiggy cover the shrub provides.

**Garden merit:** The Wall-spray or *Cotoneaster horizontalis* is probably the best-known garden Cotoneaster and will train well against a wall as its name suggests. It also makes a dense, sprawling shrub and will be happy in almost any soil or aspect. I'm very fond of *Cotoneaster microphyllus*, which is slow growing and small with dusty berries in autumn – perfect for the tiny garden. At the other end of the scale, some of the large multi-stem tree and shrub forms, such as the lovely *Cotoneaster lacteus* with clusters of late fruits, make quite an impact in an average-sized garden.

## SPINDLE
*Euonymus species*

The ever-useful evergreen *Euonymus* offers good cover for birds but it's the varieties that lose their leaves so spectacularly in autumn that are especially good for both the garden and birds.

**Good for:** Provides excellent nesting prospects for many birds as well as striking seedpods, which Robins, Sparrows and Blackbirds eat.

**Garden merit:** Native species such as *Euonymus europaeus* and *Euonymus atropurpureus*, the North American Wahoo, are the best for producing fruit. But there are other brilliant selections, such as *Euonymus europaeu*s 'Red Cascade' with fiery autumn colour and masses of pink and orange seedpods. Allow room, though, for these are fast growing and need some space to branch out.

## BARBERRY
*Berberis species*

Barberries range from small- to medium-sized shrubs, with some evergreen and others turning rich shades in autumn.

**Good for:** Dense and prickly, Barberries make brilliant cover and the fruits are favourites with many of the Thrush family.

**Garden merit:** With evergreen varieties such as *Berberis darwinii* and autumn colour beauties such as *Berberis thunbergii,* there's a Berberis to suit every type and style of garden. Versatile and easy to grow, Berberis make good specimen shrubs in the border or excellent mini-hedges for a more formal style of garden.
Watch out for the prickles though!

PERENNIALS AND ANNUALS

## ORNAMENTAL GRASSES
*Stipa, Pennisetum and Carex species*

Ornamental grasses look great in the flower border and there are lots of different varieties to choose from with something to suit every garden.

**Good for:** Grasses provide shelter and nesting material as well as seeds for birds such as Blue Tits. Grow some ornamental millet and that will feed many birds late in

*r: Carex species*

the season, including Sparrows. Leave the grasses to stand all winter for valuable shelter.

**Garden merit:** Grasses such as *Stipa*, *Pennisetum* and *Carex* are invaluable additions to the flower border. With their gentle, swishing stems they add movement and delicacy to set off flowering plants in the summer and, as the season wears on, their stems catch the light and frost giving brilliant autumn and winter interest to the garden.

## ICE PLANT
*Sedum species*

There are lots of varieties but no self-respecting wildlife gardener should be without *Sedum spectabile*, a good name for this brilliant and beautiful late bloomer.

**Good for:** Especially good for late-flying pollinators, especially butterflies and bees. But it's leaving the flower heads in place during the late autumn and winter that makes this a great plant for birds. Finches and other seed-eating birds may go for the seeds but really it's the shelter the stems provide for insects and other invertebrates that will pull in foraging birds.

**Garden merit:** There are lots of Sedum to choose from but the best garden plants are the statuesque *Sedum spectabile* types, or taller varieties such as *Sedum spectabile* 'Autumn Joy' – also known as 'Herbstfreude' – with its fantastic plates of rich pink flowers topping the blue-green, succulent foliage.

## SCABIOUS
*Knautia species*

There are a few different species of Scabious but Knautia is my top choice as it flowers right through summer and into the autumn without fail, producing masses of pincushion flowers on delicate stems.

**Good for:** Attracts plenty of insects into the garden, and consequently insect-eating birds to eat them. The seeds are also popular with Finches such as Bullfinches as the flowers fade.

**Garden merit:** Great for filling in gaps in a sunny border, Knautia will quickly fill out a space in a charming but sprawling fashion. It also looks great in 'wild' planting schemes, producing masses of flowers in pink, magenta or burgundy. The best-known variety is the lovely *Knautia macedonica* 'Melton Pastels' but my favourite is *Knautia macedonica* with its rich magenta flowers, that are also incredibly popular with bees and butterflies.

*r: Scabious*

## MICHAELMAS DAISY
*Aster, Symphyotrichum species*

Michaelmas Daisies come in all sizes and a myriad of jewel hues, adding a splash of brilliant colour late in the season.

**Good for:** Those late flowers are a good food source for many insects and, if you leave the stems after the flowers have faded, the tiny seeds are good for seed-eating birds. Wrens and Blue Tits will also use the shelter of the stems to forage for insects into the winter.

**Garden merit:** There is such a variety to choose from that there should be something to suit every garden – with some over 1 metre (3 feet) tall and others as short as 30 centimetres (12 inches). Plant them in the border, especially with grasses and other late-flowering perennials. I love *Aster amellus* varieties,especially 'King George' with its dusky blue, yellow-centred daisies that are a favourite with butterflies.

*r: Michaelmas Daisy*

## BURNET
*Sanguisorba species*

With their lovely foliage and jaunty flowers, the Burnets are brilliant plants for the border – and for birds too.

**Good for:** All sorts of insects and pollinators are drawn to the flowers, which will in turn attract birds through the summer, but it's the sturdy heads packed with seed that will feed the birds as autumn turns into winter. They will pull in seed-eating birds such as Finches, while the sheltering stems provide a foraging ground for insect eaters such as Wrens.

**Garden merit:** Burnets make a great addition to any garden. They range in size from a dainty 30 centimetres (12 inches) tall to well over 1.5 metres (5 feet), offering something to suit even the smallest of spaces. For larger gardens, choose the bright red buttons of 'Arnhem' or the fluffy heads of *Sanguisorba hakusanensis*, especially the flamboyant 'Lilac Squirrel', which will make a big impact in the border.

# BUYING BIRD FOOD

Autumn is a great time to add some shop-bought food to the plant offerings in your garden. Hopefully a few well-placed feeders and a tasty selection of grains and suet will attract the birds and keep them coming back through the winter months. Go to any garden centre and you'll be overwhelmed with the array of different bird foods and feeders on offer. While it's all a bit confusing, there are a few basic types of feed to choose from, based on the birds that will eat them. Once you've made the food selection, that will dictate the type of feeder you need.

**CLASSIC MIX:** Mainly barley, oats and other seeds that can be used in tube feeders, on the ground or on the bird table all year round.

**HIGH-ENERGY MIX:** Perfect for the breeding season, with lots of protein such as sunflower hearts and chopped peanuts.

**NIGER SEEDS:** Brilliant for Finches but very fine so they need their own special feeder, or use them on a bird table.

**PEANUTS:** Always use peanuts specially prepared for birds, as these are unsalted and shelled. Put them in a mesh feeder where birds such as Coal Tits or even Woodpeckers can peck at them. Put them out all year round, but especially in the winter months.

**MEALWORMS:** Wherever you put dried mealworms – on the bird table or added to a mix – Robins and Blackbirds will love them. In the breeding season soak them with a little water to make them easier for baby birds to digest.

*from left to right: Blue Tit, Robin, Coal Tit*

**SUET BALLS AND PELLETS:** Suet balls and blocks are a gourmet mix of fat, grains, seeds and sometimes insects that appeals to most birds, especially in winter; you can buy special suet feeders for these. Suet pellets are easy to add into mixes or place on the bird table and come flavoured with berries or insects, appealing to a wide range of birds.

# BLUE TITS AND GREAT TITS

The Tit family, or Titmouse family as they are known in the USA, really bring the garden to life with their liveliness and activity. These jaunty birds spend their lives flitting from tree to shrub in social groups and pairs, feeding on insects and feeders, chirping and singing, and nesting readily in boxes and other spots in domestic gardens. Spotting them is easy because both Blue Tits and Great Tits have beautiful yellow breasts – but Great Tits are much, much bigger than Blue Tits. Blue Tits might be small but they're colourful and lively and will eat almost anything, often hanging acrobatically from feeders. You'll see these little birds boldly tearing the papery bark off a tree to get to the insects underneath and I can remember how, back in the day when we had doorstep milk deliveries, Blue Tits would peck through the foil bottle caps to get at the tasty cream. Most Blue Tits stay in the same area year-round but, in the autumn, you'll often see flocks of them, along with other Tits, roving from garden to garden, shrub to bird table. In fact, Blue and Great Tits are some of the most frequent visitors to bird tables.

One of the most distinctive songs to make out in the garden is that of the Great Tit. I often hear it first in spring; that rhythmic 'tea-cher, tea-cher' call is instantly recognizable once your ear is tuned in.

When it comes to nesting, Tits aren't too fussy. They'll nest in some odd places, such as watering cans, a letterbox, or even an old boot, but they'll also live in old, holey trees and are often attracted to nest boxes in gardens.

*r: Great Tits, Blue Tits*

CHAPTER EIGHT

# WINTER BIRDS AND PLANTS

Winter might seem a bleak time for the garden but it's brilliant for bird watching. Small birds are often far more visible among the bare branches now the leaf cover has gone and, as they become bolder in search of food, they'll often risk coming closer to the house. That makes winter by far the best time to feed the birds – they desperately need the sustenance and will inevitably be drawn closer if you provide a safe environment. Regularly stocking up is the key thing to do as, once the birds know there's a nice safe table with plenty of foodstuffs available, they will keep coming back time after time.

While many birds migrate to the warmer temperatures, many stay at home and can face a struggle to survive the winter – especially the smaller ones. Your feeders, as well as the plants within your garden, can make the difference between life and death. Resident populations often tend to rise in the winter as many birds are drawn in to the warmer temperatures of the town, as well as from overseas – for example, the population of Robins in the UK increases during the winter months. The crucial thing is not to do too much in the garden. A light hand when tidying up and cutting back is by far the best way to help birds through these difficult months. Although your resident Robin will be very grateful if you decide to turn the compost heap or do some mulching, shadowing you to pick out any insects as they appear.

# WINTER BIRDS YOU'RE LIKELY TO SEE

During especially cold weather, when ponds and rivers are frozen in the countryside, you might get unusual garden visitors such as Grey Herons and Kingfishers.

Woodland species such as Jays, Nuthatches and Treecreepers often appear in gardens during the winter in search of food, while Fieldfares and Redwings and flocks of small birds such as Tits may pass through.

As the days start to lengthen, wintering birds such as Long-tailed Tits, Starlings, Chaffinches and Greenfinches often come into the garden from the wider countryside in search of seeds.

## THINGS TO DO

• More a list of things not to do! Leave things alone in the border. Don't cut back any late-flowering perennials until late winter if you can possibly help it. There are some things such as *Sedum* that end up a soggy mess eventually, so by all means cut that back when the time comes. But many plants will stay sturdy and upright, offering shelter for small birds and insects.

• Leave all those wonderful seed heads of *Echinacea*, *Sanguisorba*, *Aster* and *Rudbeckia* until midwinter. Seed-eating birds will nibble their way through them as winter progresses.

• Leave any leftover Apples and Pears and other fruit for the birds. It doesn't matter whether you put them on the bird table or leave them as they are, the birds will find them.

# GARDEN PLANTS FOR WINTER

## FIRETHORN
*Pyracantha species*

You may hate the thorns of *Pyracantha* but smaller birds absolutely love the dense shelter this twiggy, thorny shrub offers in nesting season.

**Good for:** While you would think the berries are the main attraction – and they are a big pull for berry-eating birds – Firethorn is hard to beat as a nesting habitat for birds such as Thrushes and Blackbirds, as well as smaller birds that feel secure in the dense, thorny maze of branches.

**Garden merit:** Besides the obvious attraction of the brilliant red or orange berries, this is such a versatile garden plant. It's evergreen and you can trim it as a hedge – it makes brilliant boundary planting with its thorny growth. Or grow it as a loose shrub – my favourite way. Admittedly it does get big and needs a firm hand with pruning, but it's swathed in creamy flowers in early summer followed by bunches of berries. It also looks fantastic trained against a wall, even a dark and cold one, where it will do wonders to brighten up the area and still provide that valuable nesting space.

## HOLLY/AMERICAN WINTERBERRY
*Ilex species*

It doesn't matter whether it's a cultivated variety or native species; as long as your Holly bears fruit it's a

*r: Holly*

winner for birds. Even the non-fruit-bearing varieties are great for nesting and shelter, but if you're planting from scratch go for fruit every time.

**Good for:** Song Thrushes, Blackbirds, Fieldfares and Redwings will feed on the fruit as winter settles in. With its dense, twiggy growth, Holly is a haven for nesting birds.

**Garden merit:** There are many Holly species and varieties to choose from but some bear fruit and others don't, so make sure you go for female varieties that fruit. One of my top ornamental choices is *Ilex x altaclerensis* 'Golden King' which, contrary to its name, is a female and has almost thornless, brightly variegated leaves and plenty of berries. The American Winterberry, *Ilex verticillata*, is a form of Holly that loses its foliage in winter, leaving the brilliant red berries on bare twigs – great for both flower arrangers and birds.

## CRAB APPLE

*Malus species*

A quick glance at the masses of little fruits will tell you that this is related to the cultivated Apple. After a froth of blossom in late spring, the autumn fruits might be smaller and harder than eating apples but they are still a magnet for insects and birds. The fruits look great in the winter garden and last well – it takes a few cold spells to soften them enough to appeal to birds.

**Good for:** Spring blossom attracts insects while the fruits attract Thrushes, Blackbirds and Crows, as well as American Robins and Cedar Waxwings in the US.

**Garden merit:** The flowering Crab Apple, *Malus floribunda*, is a beautiful garden tree and is swathed with pink and white blossom in late spring, followed by small fruits in summer. Later-fruiting Crab Apples include *Malus x zumi* 'Golden Hornet' with yellow fruits and *Malus x robusta* 'Red Sentinel' with masses of bright red 'apples', which stay on the tree well into winter.

## IVY

*Hedera species*

As well as a useful evergreen climber, Ivy is a top plant for wildlife in general. Keep it within bounds, though, or it can get out of hand.

**Good for:** The autumn flowers are a huge attraction for many bees and other insects but it's those clusters of black berries, lasting well into the winter, that provide a brilliant food source for Thrushes, Blackcaps and Blackbirds when it's most needed. Many small birds like Robins and Sparrows also love to nest in the dense growth that Ivy offers.

*r: Crab Apple*

**Garden merit:** There are some beautiful ivy varieties to choose from but many cultivated forms are reluctant to flower and fruit. Go for the classic English Ivy, *Hedera helix*, for flowers and fruit – but be warned it does need space – or look out for *Hedera helix* 'Arborescens', a non-climbing, bushy form that flowers and fruits readily and at a smaller size. Attractive climbing forms include *Hedera helix* 'Parsley Crested', with shiny, crisped leaves and *Hedera helix* 'Glacier' with small variegated white and green leaves.

## FOUNTAIN GRASS
*Pennisetum species*

This beautiful flowering grass looks good all summer but comes into its own in winter, as it holds on to its seed heads, catching spiders' webs and frosts to light up the garden.

**Good for:** Super for shelter and foraging cover for small birds such as Blue Tits and Wrens.

**Garden merit:** There are several stunning varieties to choose from but they need a sunny, warm spot to really thrive. Plant them where you can appreciate the winter interest from a window, as they will only need cutting back in early spring. *Pennisetum orientale* 'Karley Rose' has pink tufted flowers and is hardier than some varieties, while *Pennisetum alopecuroides* 'Hameln' is a compact variety that looks good all winter long.

## TURKISH SAGE

*Phlomis species*

This is one of those plants that is virtually indestructible, flowering all summer long and then leaving statuesque stems that are sturdy enough to survive the winter.

**Good for:** The summer-long flowers are great for insects, while the seeds provide food for birds such as Goldfinches and Siskins.

**Garden merit:** Tolerant of poor soil, *Phlomis russeliana* will romp away and provide masses of soft yellow flowers from late spring until the end of summer. Arguably it's even better in the autumn and winter when those sturdy stems, with their shapely seed heads at intervals up the stem, catch the frost and the light beautifully. Allow it some room to be architectural, but do weed out any seedlings or it might take over the garden.

## TEASELS

*Dipsacus species*

These are easy to grow and self-seed freely, which has led to them being regarded as somewhat invasive in the USA.

*r: Turkish Sage*

**Good for:** The spiny stems offer protection for lots of wildlife and bees and other insects love the flowers, while Goldfinches feed on the seeds.

**Garden merit:** These striking thistle-like plants with their gentle mauve flowers are brilliant for adding height to the border in summer, standing tall above perennials. In winter their structure and shape make them stand out, especially when covered in frost.

## CARDOON
*Cynara cardunculus*

While it's not a plant for the small garden, the huge neon flowers of Cardoon make it a favourite for those with a bit more room.

**Good for:** A plant abuzz with bees in summer, it's the seed heads and stems that offer the best value for birds. Those huge flowers turn into soft, fibrous seed heads, which provide seeds as well as fluffy nesting material, while the thick stems are a haven for birds to hunt insects.

**Garden merit:** Tall and imposing, these thistles are a great addition to the border, both for their lovely silver foliage and their fantastic, bright blue flowers. They need room, though, so be warned – and they can topple over in strong winds. I cut mine back in autumn as they tend to get too top heavy, but leave the seed heads on the wall for the birds to take.

# BIRD TABLES

There are lots of ways to feed birds, even if your garden is tiny – the obvious method is to hang feeders in trees or from a pole. But a bird table gives you some great advantages over hanging feeders; not only does it let you have several different foods in one spot, hopefully attracting a wider variety of birds, but also to hang feeders from it and, if it has a roof, to provide shelter for the birds and food too. The classic bird table is freestanding on a pole fixed to the ground, but you can also fix it to a wall or fence post – making sure it's not accessible to any neighbouring cats of course – or you can use a hanging bird table. There are plenty of different styles around, but it doesn't need to be anything fancy – as long as it's secure, safe and sheltered.

Keep your bird table and feeders clean and regularly refilled. Once you start feeding birds, it's important to keep going because the birds come to expect it and, if you don't supply food, they'll go elsewhere.

## MAKE YOUR OWN TABLE

Use wood that won't fall apart or disintegrate, such as outdoor-quality plywood.

Make the table about 30 x 50 centimetres (12 x 20 inches) – you can go bigger if you want – and about 1 centimetre (½ inches) thick. Fix some sort of rim – a piece of baton will do – around the edge, leaving gaps at the corners for cleaning and so the rain can run off. This will stop messy birds or the wind tumbling food over the edge.

Simply hang the platform from chains or support it on a pole, and add a couple of hooks to hang feeders from, and perhaps a roof if you're getting creative.

## LOCATION TIPS

Location is key and it might take a couple of tries before you get the right spot.

• In the open enough to deter cats.

• Near enough to perches such as shrubs and trees for birds to get to it easily.

• Visible from your window so you can see the birds that visit.

# ROBINS

Robins are the first birds we ever learn to recognize, with their distinctive red breasts and chirpy, lively singing. They're also so easy to spot in your garden, not only because of their red breasts, which both the male and female have, but also because of their bold, fearless attitude. Robins are very territorial, each claiming a sector or garden of their own and defending their claim loudly and bravely. I've even seen a parent Robin successfully warning off a cat that was getting too close to its nest, succeeding through sheer ferocity.

Robins will famously nest almost anywhere – an old teapot hanging in a tree will do – and they're a true 'gardener's friend', keeping you company all winter long as you work in the garden, hoping to grab a few tasty morsels as you weed, dig and mulch. They'll sing their hearts out all winter, too, which is such a joy on a cold day – that's because, unusually for many birds, they protect their territory all year round.

The American Robin, despite its red breast, is a type of Thrush and, as you might expect, has a beautiful song that people love. Unlike the European Robin, which you'll only ever see on its own or in pairs, the American Robin often gathers in large roosts of hundreds of birds. While the European Robin is for many a key bird of winter – featuring in carols, Christmas cards and the like – for Americans, the Robin's singing heralds spring days.

*l: Robin ♂*

CHAPTER NINE

# SPOTTING
# BIRDS

Once you start really looking at the birds that visit your garden, you quickly realize some are around every bit as often as you are, all year round, come rain or shine. These birds are often the ones you get to know first, simply because you see each other so often – like commuters at a railway station. Birds such as the Robin and the nervous Blackbird couple, the cautious little Wren and the ponderous Pigeon. These common birds are the ones that are most likely to make themselves at home in your garden, feeding, mating, nesting and bringing up their chicks without venturing too far from your patch. Keeping an eye on the parts these birds favour and their habits means that you can make subtle improvements to make your garden even more attractive and welcoming. Make these birds at home and you're well on the way to encouraging other, more fleeting visitors, to stop and feed.

All gardens can attract lots of different birds, but what can you expect to see on the bird feeder? Common species include a range of Finches and Tits, also Robins, Dunnocks, Blackbirds and Starlings. Suburban gardens can also occasionally pull in some of the birds you'd expect to see in the wider countryside as infrequent visitors, such as Nuthatches, Siskins and Woodpeckers. In autumn and winter, you might also see 'dissimulations' of small birds, which is when smaller species, such as Long-tailed Tits, Blue Tits, Goldcrests and even Treecreepers, flock together loosely, hoping for safety in numbers as they move from garden to garden. You'll also spot birds such as Redwings, Fieldfares and sometimes Waxwings passing through the garden.

Watching birds requires patience – and some good binoculars also help! A pair with 8 x 42 magnification is best as otherwise they can prove difficult to hold steady. All you need is a good place to encourage the birds to congregate, such as a bird table or bird feeder, some good books or apps to help with identification and some patience. It's a question of taking the time to watch and learn about the birds that already visit your garden, identifying what environments they like – whether those are high perches or shrubby thickets – the foods they like and their habits. For example, Treecreepers are slim and brown and blend into the bark of the trees they climb up looking for insects; it takes time and patience to spot them. Nuthatches are larger and more brightly coloured, with lovely soft blue and gold plumage, and while they also climb up trees, you can often spot them coming down them headfirst, too.

It's also essential to learn some of the calls, so you can narrow down the location of interesting birds. If you're working in the garden, you have the time and the quiet to pick out individual calls and a good app can help you isolate the distinctive ones. What birds want from your garden is quite simple: readily available things such as twigs, lichen, moss and mud for nest building and shelter in the form of thick hedges, shrubs, and herbaceous plants – which in turn provide seeds and insects to eat. Even the compost heap is a valuable source of insects when you're digging through it in autumn and winter.

In summer and autumn garden seeds provide brilliant fuel for birds, and many eat little else. While you can also provide seeds in your bird feeders, there is a natural abundance of seeds in the garden, from both weeds and cultivated plants. For their size and weight, seeds are highly nutritious and rather conveniently packaged, although sometimes they're hard for birds to get at because plants have become rather good at protecting them. If you think about it, while birds are brilliantly evolved for flying, they have lost useful feeding tools, such as teeth and front legs. However, beaks come in all shapes and sizes for this very reason. For instance, although the Chaffinch has a good beak for dealing with all sorts of food – spiders, caterpillars, insects, berries, picking up seeds – it's no good whatsoever for getting into an armoured seed such as a Sunflower with its tough shell. But that shell is no obstacle to the sturdy beak of the Greenfinch.

Our gardens offer the potential for great harmony between people and birds, if we take the time to look for it. All common birds were originally woodland species, but many have learned that living alongside us offers them security and a regular food supply. But we get even greater returns, not simply in the form of their insect-eating habits – so useful for managing garden pests – but in their beauty, their incomparable songs and their company, too. That sense of sharing our space with other living creatures is something we all savour about our gardens and with birds you are never alone.

*Clockwise from top: Chaffinch, Treecreeper, Greenfinch*

# FINCHES

Chaffinches, Greenfinches and Goldfinches are some of the most regular visitors to our gardens all year round. While the Goldfinch is probably the most striking with its gold and red plumage – and noisy too – it's the Chaffinch you're most likely to see, with its pink cheeks and breast. Chaffinches rival the Robin for the title of the UK's second commonest breeding bird – the Wren is the most prolific. While the male is beautifully coloured, the female is similar to a House Sparrow, and the birds often have a distinct regional variation to their songs. They're called Chaffinches because of their habit of descending on harvested fields, sorting through the chaff for seeds.

Greenfinches are large and green, as you might expect, with sturdy strong bills that are perfect for cracking open strong-shelled seeds such as Sunflowers. They have the most bizarre mating flight in the spring, flying slowly and showily while barely staying aloft, but they'll happily spend the rest of the year roosting in groups in conifers such as *Leylandii*.

*l: Chaffinch ♂ Greenfinch ♂*
*r: Goldfinch ♀ ♂*

Goldfinches are one of the UK's most spectacular garden birds and a real success story, too. As more people have become interested in feeding garden birds, the winter survival rate of Goldfinches has improved accordingly – they especially love Nyjer seeds. A group of Goldfinches is collectively known as a 'charm' and with good reason, as their delightful tinkling, twittering chatter and fluttering flashes of brilliant yellow and red as they move from one clump of Teasels or Thistles to another is utterly charming. So charming, in fact, that Goldfinches became popular caged birds and by 1890 the population was severely endangered. The newly formed Society for the Protection of Birds, which later became the RSPB, set about reversing this decline as one of its first objectives and thankfully succeeded.

# OWLS

You might not think of an Owl as a garden bird, but the chances are that your garden is part of an Owl's territory. All Owls have excellent hearing, and of course their large eyes are good for hunting day or night – although most are predominantly nocturnal. They're brilliant predators, preying on rodents mainly, and they're spookily almost silent in flight. Most owls don't build a nest of their own and will instead lay their eggs in holes on the ground or in the abandoned nests of other birds.

Tawny Owls are the commonest Owl residents in UK towns and cities, although, as they are truly nocturnal, you'll rarely see them. But you'll be familiar with the call of the Tawny Owl – that haunting 'toowit, toowoo' that you hear mainly through the winter months. That's really two birds, the male and female, doing a call and response to highlight their territory to other Owls. This is vital, as Tawny Owls rarely move more than a mile from their birthplace, so establishing their patch is crucial – especially as their fledged offspring, unwilling to travel to a new area, attempt to grab a territory of their own.

While Owls are widely considered to be nocturnal, many hunt by day or in the evening, including Little Owls. These tiny birds were introduced to the UK from continental Europe and are only about the size of a Thrush but much stockier. They hunt small mammals, earthworms, birds and insects, often at dusk and dawn, scuttling along the ground more like a Blackbird than an Owl. If you're lucky, you might spot one perched on a branch or gatepost in the garden.

*r: Barn Owl ♂*

Whether you're in Europe or the USA, spotting a ghostly pale Barn Owl – with its distinctive heart shaped face – gliding on silent wings through the night is a magical experience. Although they're mostly found in rural areas, Barn Owls are happy to make use of owl nest boxes, so you may be lucky enough to see them near your garden, especially as they will also hunt in daytime.

CHAPTER TEN

# PROBLEMS AND PREDATORS

S ometimes it can feel like you're fighting a losing battle trying to attract birds to your garden. With predators like the neighbourhood cats, urban foxes, squirrels and rats – not to mention predatory birds – your little bird populations have a lot to contend with. In truth, urban foxes rarely attack small birds – anything less than a Pigeon simply isn't worth bothering with. Squirrels and rats will take eggs and chicks, but rarely attack adult birds, which does mean those birds are able to breed again.

Pet cats are by far the main problem pest for small birds. They're born hunters and, though you might think that a cat doesn't catch many birds, the numbers still mount up – even if it only catches a bird every month or two. With something like seven million pet cats in the UK, that's somewhere between 30 and 75 million garden birds a year that get caught and killed. The problem is that those are mostly adult birds which reduces the breeding populations massively. Using a special cat deterrent that emits a high-pitched sound inaudible to humans is reputed to be effective, as is placing a bell on the collar of a cat, which helps alert the birds to their presence. But perhaps the best thing is to make your garden safe for birds with bird tables, nest boxes and thicket shrubs that are inaccessible to cats.

Cats are introduced predators, not natural ones, and, because they're well fed and looked after by their owners, they have an unnatural advantage over their prey. It's a distinct boost on the food chain. Predatory birds, on the other hand, are completely natural predators of small birds and have been hunting them for eons. Their lives are inextricably linked with their prey, enmeshed in a food chain that may be brutal to our sensibilities but is completely natural. The Grey Heron has decimated the large fish in my pond but it's still an imposing sight in my garden, and seeing a Sparrowhawk swoop down and tackle a Pigeon that's equal in size is an awesome sight.

Some birds have bad reputations for taking other birds' eggs and chicks. Certainly Magpies and, to a lesser extent Jays, are blamed for the declining numbers of many small birds. But this isn't an accurate representation of the situation. While Magpies, Jays, and even Great Spotted Woodpeckers will raid nests in the early spring when they're hungry, the reduction in song-bird populations is far more likely to be the result of modern farming practices and the consequent decline of insect food in the countryside.

I love seeing the pair of Jays that nest near my garden year after year. They're surprisingly timid birds for their size, and are beautiful with their buff-pink plumage and brilliant blue flash on the wing. I know they can sometimes raid nests but they also do an enormously valuable job in spreading oak trees through the countryside. This is because they're one of the few birds that store food for winter, by burying acorns in autumn and then forgetting where they are. Not such a villain after all.

# SPARROWHAWKS
## ...AND A WORD ON BUZZARDS

Sparrowhawks are the UK's third most common bird of prey, after Kestrels and Buzzards, and frankly you're not likely to see a Kestrel in your garden. The Sparrowhawk, on the other hand, loves urban gardens for their rich pickings, but you can also spot them around parks and leafy suburbs. They're brilliant predators, bold enough to tackle a bird their own size and, with their camouflage plumage in shades of grey and brown, they're also slick at concealing themselves in foliage, ready to pounce. This habit of sticking to the shadows means you might not know one is even there until it swoops down to grab a Blue Tit from the bird table – a good reason to make sure yours has a roof! Sparrowhawks are super quick and completely ambush smaller birds, relying on the element of surprise. The females are up to a third bigger than the males, which means they can catch bigger prey such as Pigeons, while the smaller males focus on songbirds. Good hunting all across the board.

But things have been tough for the Sparrowhawk in the recent past, although it's had something of resurgence since the 1960s when its numbers declined sharply. That was due to the use of pesticides such as DDT, which became more concentrated as they passed higher up the food chain from prey to predator. Not only did they poison the birds themselves, but they also caused the eggshells of many birds of prey to thin to breaking point and so the populations of Sparrowhawks and others, including Buzzards, plummeted. Since the chemicals have been banned, Sparrowhawks have become a common bird in our gardens.

*r: Sparrowhawk ♀*

The other bird of prey you're most likely to see around your garden is the Buzzard, the UK's largest common bird of prey. You're unlikely to see it at close quarters but they're a common sight circling high over the garden, often in pairs, calling to one another with a high-pitched plaintive 'kee kee'. Even though they're big, they don't have it all their own way, as Crows will mob them if they get too close to their territory, warning them off their patch and protecting their young.

# CROWS, MAGPIES AND JAYS

If any birds have a bad reputation, it's these three. Crows, Magpies and Jays are all generally regarded as thuggish and opportunist, stealing eggs and even chicks from other, smaller birds. This is their nature, however, and although all three will prey on nests, the effect on songbird populations is very small. Crows and Magpies have become successful in our towns and cities, mainly because of their intelligence and adaptability. Both are top-notch scavengers, making the most of Saturday night takeaways and roadkill as well as garden bird tables. Magpies are particularly bold and fearless in our gardens, and they're surprisingly handsome when you look at them closely, with their iridescent blue-black plumage and strutting, voluble cockiness.

I have a slow-grown love for Crows, having shared my garden with the same pair for some 10 years. These long-lived birds are cautious of people, rarely letting you get too close, flying up to sit in a tree and caw a loud warning in a hoarse voice. They're fierce defenders of their family, mobbing a Buzzard in flight to keep it away from the nest. Crows tend to be quite solitary; you'll see them alone or in pairs, as they often mate for life – which can be around 20 years. But it's their cleverness that really marks them out, with Crows known to drop seashells onto stones to crack them open – and research shows that Crows are even smart enough to put stones into a beaker of water to raise the level high enough to drink, just like in the fable by Greek storyteller Aesop.

The elusive Jay is one of my favourites to spot in the garden because it's a bird of the trees and shadows. Often it's just a flash of electric blue wing glimpsed out of the corner of my

*r: Jay ♀*

eye but, occasionally, I'll get the opportunity to study one as it's distracted, gathering acorns. These are the most beautiful members of the Crow family, with their dusky pink plumage, black-streaked head and those wings of black, white and electric blue. But Jays also perform a valuable service in maintaining UK woodlands. In autumn, they bury acorns to feed themselves through the lean winter months, later forgetting at least some of their cache, which then sprout into new oak trees. Studies have estimated that a Jay spends around 10 hours a day in autumn burying hundreds, if not thousands of acorns, in a few short weeks. Something to think about next time you spot a seedling oak tree.

CHAPTER ELEVEN

# RESOURCES AND READING LIST

There is a wealth of information and advice available for anyone interested in the birds in their garden. Not only are there plenty of books and websites available on birds of the UK, Europe and the wider world, but there are also identification apps for your phone. Several websites also feature snippets of birdsong to help you identify those birds you can hear but can't spot.

Finding information on the plants that birds favour is less straightforward, especially when it comes to plants that you would want to have in your garden. Here are a few books, websites and apps that may prove useful.

BOOKS
May, Derwent, *How to Attract Birds to Your Garden*
(Robson Books, 2001)

Moss, Stephen, *Gardening for Birds*
(Harper Collins, 2000)

Svensson, Lars, *Collins Bird Guide: The Most Complete Guide to the Birds of Britain and Europe* (Collins, 2010)

Westwood, Brett and Moss, Stephen, *Tweet of the Day*
(Hodder & Stoughton, 2014)

WEBSITES
**Royal Society for the Protection of Birds** rspb.org.uk
Great UK website that contains all you need to know about birds and their habits, plus an incredibly useful birdsong identification section (at rspb.org.uk/birds-and-wildlife/bird-songs/what-bird-is-that).

**British Garden Birds** garden-birds.co.uk
Useful guide to watching and identifying UK garden birds.
Includes tips on ways to make birds at home in your garden.

**Birdspot** birdspot.co.uk
Easy-to-use website with lots of ideas for making your garden
more bird friendly.

**Royal Horticultural Society** rhs.org.uk
UK website with plenty of useful information on gardening and
plants in general, plus specific advice on gardening for birds.

**Birds and Blooms** birdsandblooms.com
US website with lovely ideas for gardening for birds and wildlife
in general.

**The Cornell Lab of Ornithology** birds.cornell.edu
US website with a wealth of information about birds, their
habitats and getting involved with citizen science projects.

**National Audubon Society** audubon.org
US association for the protection of birds and their habitats
across the Americas. Useful information on birds and
suggestions on native plants for different areas.

APPS

**eGuide to British Birds RSPB**
Interactive companion to *RSPB Handbook of British Birds*.

**iBird UK Pro Guide to Birds**
Offers a great feature called Birds Around Me, or BAM,
that shows only birds found in your GPS area, making
identification easier.

**Birds of Britain Pocket Guide**
Great photos, songs and packed with information and
interesting facts.

**Merlin Bird ID Cornell Lab**
Covers worldwide birds by location, time of year and song.

**BirdID Nord University**
Norwegian app also available in English.

**Audubon Bird Guide National Audubon Society**
Field guide to over 800 North American birds.

# INDEX OF COMMON AND LATIN NAMES

Blue Tit (Titmouse) *Cyanistes caeruleus*
Bluebird *Sialia* species
Brown Flycatcher *Muscicapa dauurica*
Bullfinch *Pyrrhula pyrrhula*
Burnet *Sanguisorba* species
Buzzard *Buteo buteo*

## C

Cardoon *Cynara cardunculus*
Chaffinch *Fringilla coelebs*
Cherry *Prunus* species
Clematis *Clematis* species
Clover *Trifolium* species
Coal Tit (Titmouse) *Periarus ater*
Collared Dove *Streptopelia decaocto*
Coneflower *Echinacea* species
Coot *Fulica atra*
Cornflower *Centaurea cyanus*
Cotoneaster *Cotoneaster* species
Cow Parsley *Anthriscus sylvestris*
Crab Apple *Malus* species
Crow *Corvus corone*
Cuckoo *Cuculus canorus*

## D

Daisy *Bellis* species
Dandelion *Taraxacum officinale*
Dogwood *Cornus* species
Downy Woodpecker *Dryobates pubescens*

Dunnock (Hedge Sparrow) *Prunella modularis*

## E

Elder *Sambucus nigra*
European Robin *Erithacus rubecula*
Evening Primrose *Oenothera biennis*

## F

False Indigo *Baptisia australis*
Fennel *Foeniculum vulgare*
Feral Pigeon *Columba livia*
Fieldfare *Turdus pilaris*
Firecrest *Regulus ignicapillus*
Firethorn *Pyracantha* species
Fountain Grass *Pennisetum* species

## G

Garden Warbler *Sylvia borin*
Giant Oat Grass *Stipa gigantea*
Globe Thistle *Echinops species*
Goldcrest *Regulus regulus*
Golden Oriole *Oriolus oriolus*
Goldenrod *Solidago* species
Goldfinch *Carduelis carduelis*
Great Tit (Titmouse) *Parus major*
Great Spotted Woodpecker *Dendrocopus major*
Green Woodpecker *Picus viridis*
Greenfinch *Carduelis chloris*
Grey Heron *Ardea cinerea*
Guelder Rose *Viburnum* species

## H

Hawthorn *Crataegus* species
Holly *Ilex* species
Honeysuckle *Lonicera* species
Hooded Pitohui *Pitohui dichrous*
House Finch *Haemorhous mexicanus*
House Martin *Delichon urbica*
House Sparrow *Passer domesticus*

## I

Ice Plant *Sedum* species
Ivy *Hedera* species

## J

Jay *Garrulus glandarius*

## K

Kalonji *Nigella sativa*
Kestrel *Falco tinnunculus*
Kingfisher *Alcedo atthis*

## L

Lavender *Lavendula* species
Lesser Spotted Woodpecker
    *Dendrocopus minor*
Leylandii species *X cupressocyparis leylandii*
Linnet *Carduelis cannabina*
Little Owl *Athene noctua*
Loganberry *Rubus x loganobaccus*
Long-tailed Tit (Titmouse)
    *Aegithalos caudatus*
Love-in-a-Mist *Nigella* species

## M

Magpie *Pica pica*
Marjoram *Origanum majorana*
Meadowsweet *Spiraea* species
Michaelmas Daisy *Symphyotrichum, Aster* species
Mint *Mentha spicata*
Mistle Thrush *Turdus viscivorus*
Mistletoe V*iscum album*
Mockingbird *Mimus polyglottos*
Moorhen *Gallinula chloropus*
Mourning Dove *Zenaida macroura*

## N

Nasturtium *Tropaeolum majus*
North American Wahoo *Euonymus atropurpureus*
Northern Cardinal *Cardinalis cardinalis*
Nuthatch *Sitta europaea*

## O

Oak *Quercus* species

## P

Pear *Pyrus* species
Peregrine Falcon *Falco peregrinus*
Pied Wagtail *Motacilla alba*
Plum *Prunus* species

## R

Raven *Corvus corax*
Redcurrant *Ribes rubrum*
Redwing *Turdus iliacus*
Rock Pigeon *Columba livia*
Rose *Rosa* species
Rosemary *Rosmarinus officinalis*
Rowan *Sorbus* species

## S

Scabious *Knautia* species
Sea Holly *Eryngium* species
Sedge Grass *Carex* species
Selfheal *Prunella vulgaris*
Serviceberry *Amelanchier* species
Siskin *Carduelis spinus*
Snowy Mespilus *Amelanchier lamarckii*
Song Thrush *Turdus philomelos*
Sparrowhawk *Accipiter nisus*
Spindle *Euonymus* species
Spirea *Spiraea* species
Spotted Flycatcher *Muscicapa striata*
Starling *Sturnus vulgaris*
Stellar's Jay *Cyanocitta stelleri*
Sunflower *Helianthus* species
Swallow *Hirundo rustica*
Sweet Pea *Lathyrus odoratus*
Swift *Apus apus*

## T

Tawny Owl *Strix aluco*
Teasels *Dipsacus* species
Towhee *Pipilo erythrophthalmus*
Tree Sparrow *Passer montanus*
Treecreeper *Certhia familiaris*
Tufted Titmouse *Baeolophus bicolor*
Turkish Sage *Phlomis* species

## W

Waxwing *Bombycilla garrulus*
White-breasted Nuthatch *Sitta carolinensis*
Wisteria *Wisteria* species
Wood Pigeon *Columba palumbus*
Wren *Troglodytes troglodytes*

# ACKNOWLEDGEMENTS

My name might be on the cover, but it's the beautiful illustrations of James Weston Lewis that catch the eye, for which I thank him from the bottom of my heart. Thank you, James.

All books are a collaborative effort, and my thanks also go to the marvellous Harriet Butt, Maeve Bargman and the rest of the Quadrille team – it's a joy working with you.

A 'thank you' is simply not enough for Jane Graham Maw and Maddy Belton from Graham Maw Christie for their constant support and unwavering enthusiasm but it will have to suffice – thank you both.

For all the bird knowhow I could ever want and more besides, thanks to Haydn, Annie and my mum Theo for all their ideas, observations and thoughts. I hope you all approve.

# ABOUT THE AUTHOR

In a horticultural career spanning 30 years, Jane Moore has been head gardener at a Benedictine abbey, a writer for national gardening magazines and newspapers, a researcher on BBC gardening programmes and a presenter on BBC TV's *Gardeners' World*. Gardening, and writing about gardening, has encompassed Jane's whole career. She has wide-ranging practical experience, an astonishingly broad plant knowledge and an unswerving enthusiasm for gardens, horticulture and their impact on everyday life. She has also published *Planting for Butterflies* (2020) and *Planting for Wildlife* (2021).

**Managing Director** Sarah Lavelle
**Senior Commissioning Editor** Harriet Butt
**Assistant Editor** Oreolu Grillo
**Series Designer** Maeve Bargman
**Illustrator** James Weston Lewis
**Head of Production** Stephen Lang
**Production Controller** Nikolaus Ginelli

Published in 2022 by **Quadrille**,
an imprint of **Hardie Grant Publishing**

Quadrille
52–54 Southwark Street
London SE1 1UN
**quadrille.com**

**Cataloguing in Publication Data:** a catalogue record
for this book is available from the British Library.

ISBN 978 178713 8292

Reprinted in 2022, 2023
10 9 8 7 6 5 4 3

Printed in China using soy inks

*Firecrest* ♂